From Toxic Civil Discourse to Saving a World

From TOXIC CIVIL DISCOURSE *to* SAVING A WORLD

A Midrash-Guided Memoir of a Vietnam Vet

LAWRENCE H. CLIMO, M.D.

KTAV Publishing House
New York

From Toxic Civil Discourse *to* Saving a World:
A Midrash-Guided Memoir of a Vietnam Vet

by Lawrence H. Climo, M.D.

Typeset by Juliet Tresgallo

Printed in Israel
First Edition
ISBN 978-965-524-374-1

KTAV Publishing House
527 Empire Boulevard
Brooklyn, NY 11225
www.ktav.com

Urim Publications
P.O. Box 52287
Jerusalem 9152102, Israel
www.UrimPublications.com

CONTENTS

INTRODUCTION

This is a personal story, a memoir. I'd become tired of indulging my nation's divisive and toxic civil discourse and then feeling guilty; but then indulging it again, back and forth and over and over. I wished, of course, I could do something about that toxicity but it was overwhelming.

My reflections about the current toxic split in America's discourse reminded me of an earlier split that took place years before. Back then, the split was inside me, pulling me in two directions, and it became a crisis because it forced me to betray ethical standards and corrupt my integrity, all taking place during the Vietnam War era. And while that was happening to me another split was taking place, this other one a national split. Americans were disagreeing on whether or not we should be in Vietnam fighting. Those two splits back then, mine and America's were, of course, different. America's split was between one American and another American. Mine was between one part of me and another part of me. (That personal split, I should point out, is where this memoir begins.)

As to whether that split I suffered back then or even the nation's split over that war, had any direct connection with our current civil discourse, I can't say. What I can say is that that long ago experience prepared me, not for picking a side and winning but for picking a side and living with that split comfortably and peacefully because that's what it did and it worked for a long time. Today's toxic divisiveness and our adjustment to it, in comparison, prepares us more for its gradual increases in violence, than ways to live comfortably with our differences. I can also say that nobody today seems particularly interested in, let alone able to, fix or stop it and make it go away. There was certainly nothing I could do. Who was I to tackle it anyway? It wasn't just that I had no credentials. Fundamentally, I was of two minds on the matter. So, I just continued my cycle of participating, indulging, and feeling guilty.

It was at this time I began reading a book, given as a gift from my Rabbi (Dr. Robert Goldstein of Temple Emanuel in Andover, MA), a book edited by a college classmate (Rabbi, Ph.D., and Steinberg Emeritus Professor, Dr. William Cutter of Hebrew Union College) "Midrash & Medicine: Healing Body and Soul in the Jewish Interpretive Tradition" from which ideas uncannily slipped into my awareness hinting at ways to approach my personal issues and even appreciate a way out. It was not long after this that my mounting frustration and the escalating toxicity of our civil discourse led me first to revisit a familiar Talmudic statement (Sanhedrin 37a) that says: "Whoever saves a single life is considered by scripture to have saved the whole world." I, being me back then – and someone for whom writing has long been a slow-motion version of talking to myself – read that statement as a metaphor.

What unfolded, I was heartened to discover, was a widening and deepening interpretation of those words which, in turn, led me from, "If one saves A life, one saves THE whole world" to, "If one saves ONE'S OWN life one saves A whole world" to "If one FULFILLS ONE'S OWN LIFE one CAN save ANOTHER'S world." It seemed I'd found a handle on my issue along with a path forward. Those Midrash readings in Dr. Cutter's book that had initially touched me only as perceptive and instructive perspectives, had become genuine insights and essentially colleagues and partners.

Things moved quickly. I ignored the concept of "credentials," replaced it with "mindset" and "attitude," and from there refocused my attention, not on what I might do about being of two minds, but on what I must try *not* to do with either of those minds. Unfortunately, that concept, *not* to do, is an undertaking that has no clear title, and "doing nothing" is still tagged with monikers like "lazy," "cowardly," and "chicken." Likewise, time spent reflecting and pondering is still confused with "inattentiveness," "absentmindedness," and sometimes "spacing out." But, because I am a professional healer by trade, my specialty being mental healing – I'm a psychiatrist – and because my view of our toxic divisiveness had been as if an illness, a national malady in need of healing, I did have that familiar and user-friendly medical frame-of-reference, as a starting overview.

I already had a starting point, of course. I'd kept a diary and had already published a book about those personal experiences during the Vietnam War era. I'd been opposed to that War but served anyway, meaning I'm a Vietnam Vet who stood on both sides of that divide, a foot in each camp. (This was when I found myself torn in two.) I was a general doctor in the American

Army just out of medical internship and volunteered in basic training for a unique State Department mission wherein I'd be assigned to the Republic of Vietnam Health Service, and would be treating Vietnamese civilians exclusively, and would be responsible to their Ministry of Health. I would not be treating Americans, just sick and hurting Vietnamese civilians. My perspective, therefore, would be unusually broad and remarkably unique inasmuch as I was not only witness to toxic seeds being sown back then, I was myself a sower of those seeds.

I did, however, have one other asset. I knew that for this task and this memoir, I'd have to be open-minded. I knew I had to conscientiously think outside the box. But, I also knew that thinking outside the box had always come easily to me; it was thinking *inside* the box that had given me trouble. In Bible studies, which I always enjoyed attending, there was never any box to think inside of. And, as the Tanakh, the Jewish Bible, was arguably the world's oldest "How-To-Live-In-Our-Imperfect-World-And-Make-It-Work" manual, and given that the tradition of commentary about those texts had essentially been those of course correction throughout life, I knew from Dr. Cutter's book that I'd be re-reading and referencing some of those intriguing signposts, those early and also temporary *Midrashim*. There was depth, breadth, and a sense of liberation now to my outlook and musings. Midrash, both early and temporary, had broadened my outlook and enriched and liberated me enough to go forward with this memoir of saving a world, one person's world at a time, starting with the other guy's.

That said, and expecting my readers to be of two minds just as I was and still am – i.e. that *not* being an issue – and this book being the slo-mo process that took me to the solution, I'll explain the solution now in simple language. This memoir is the story of a journey – mine – which can very well be yours as well. It's a nation's story. It's a journey getting into something but also getting out of that something. The solution? *Show respect to others.*

My journey towards that solution, simple, effortless, and dismissible, officially began, not with my wishing and griping, but my digesting the following.

Midrash on Deuteronomy 22:1–3, Restoring Possessions

"If you see your fellow's ox or sheep gone astray, do not ignore it; you must take it back to your fellow. If your fellow does not live near you or you do not know who he is, you shall bring it home and it shall remain with you until your fellow claims it; then you shall give it back to him. You shall do the same with his ass; you shall do the same with his garment; and so too shall you do with anything that your fellow loses and you find: you must not remain indifferent."

Then, there's this: Moses Maimonides, writing in the twelfth century about restoring lost possessions to their owner, interprets those verses as encompassing the physician's obligation "to heal the sick."[1] Maimonides is here expanding the reach of the scriptural phrase, "and you shall restore it to him" to include restoring to someone his lost health. Rabbi Simkha Weintraub, writing in the 21st century and referencing this Maimonides comment, extends its reach, if not obligation, to include in its commission everyone who works to help and heal those who suffer, to help them recover their lost health, not just physicians.[2]

My 21ˢᵗ Century Midrash Takeaway

While we are all, at periods or moments in our lives, not just caring but also caregivers, anyone and everyone falls within this purview of those obliged to try to help restore to someone his or her lost health, in his or her world. Or, in this instance, help restore to all of us our lost health.

1. Maimonides, Mishnah Commentary on Nedarim 4:4 quoted by Rabbi Simkha Y. Weintraub, PhD, in *Midrash & Medicine: Healing Body and Soul in the Jewish Interpretive Tradition*, by Rabbi William Cutter, PhD, Editor (Vermont: Jewish Lights Publishing, 2011), pp. 10–11.

2. Rabbi Simkha Y. Weintraub, PhD, in *Midrash & Medicine: Healing Body and Soul in the Jewish Interpretive Tradition*, by Rabbi William Cutter, PhD, Editor (Vermont: Jewish Lights Publishing, 2011), pp. 10–11.

PART I:

A MEMORABLE COLLAPSE
OF ETHICS AND INTEGRITY

CHAPTER 1

MY PERSONAL STORY – AMERICA'S STORY

Parallel trajectories: An omen

My Vietnam experience of being assigned to the Vietnamese Government Health Service as part of a State Department counter-insurgency program (that to this day no one has heard of) – a mission I'd volunteered for in Army Basic Training – turned out to be neither unique nor problematic to me alone. It uncannily paralleled our nation's experience and, in doing so, became like a personal portal into that experience, a portal that never closed. We were both trapped. What happened next was, for us both, painfully personal and shamefully true.

I'll begin with this memory: There was an isolated Montagnard village near the Cambodian border in need of supplies. The Special Forces camp where I was staying at the time had those supplies and wanted to bring them. This village was non-aligned and it was important there be an American connection. The Special Forces captain asked me to go along because that village was outside the range and beyond the reach of the Vietnamese public health facilities, so I could represent a Saigon government outreach. We couldn't go by truck; there were no roads, only paths and trails. We couldn't go by jeep; there were streams and no bridges. And, we couldn't go by air; there was no helicopter. We went by elephant. There were a total of seven elephants in our convoy. Three hours into the trip we suddenly became engulfed in smoke. Something was on fire. The elephants became frightened and ran. They scattered. By the time my elephant handler guided our animal to safety, there were no other elephants in sight and we couldn't see the trail. What had happened was, the day before, a team of Special Forces Montagnard scouts had gone ahead to identify the most likely site for an enemy ambush with orders to neutralize it, and had found such a site, and set it on fire. That was the source of the smoke; the fire was still smoldering. The captain's counter-ambush strategy had literally backfired.

With that story in mind I can say: We – America and I – were both dragged into a war neither of us wanted and about which we were slow in catching on. We were both on a steep learning curve and continually playing catchup in the face of speed bumps and snares (and backfires). We were both making tough moral choices that we had to learn to live with as we soldiered on. We soldiered on for the right reasons but with the wrong understanding and so guilt and remorse added to the things we carried. We both had cause to feel confident and both ended up doing more harm than good. We were both, in a sense, going it alone. Like that elephant convoy, we both started on a "high horse" only to end up in a thicket, a thicket that was smoldering and the visibility poor. You couldn't see where the trail ended; couldn't even see if there was an end to the trail, but you couldn't just stop, get off, and walk away. You'd get burned. But neither could you stay on and expect to end up where you set out to go.

CHAPTER 2

ETHICAL CLASHES SPARK MY BETRAYAL

A toxic division inside me materializes

My mission and purpose were clear. Like that of America's military mission and purpose in Vietnam, mine was to help create a strong, lasting, non-communist Saigon government. I was there to win the hearts and minds of the people to their government so they'd stop providing sanctuary to the Vietcong among them. I'd accomplish this by augmenting the government's depleted and dysfunctional public health system. Most of their doctors had been drafted into their army. In this way, I'd show the people that their Saigon government still cared for them despite its appearance of distance, aloofness, corruption, and repression. The people would then invest their allegiance into Saigon and legitimize and strengthen that authority.

My orders were explicit. Support customary Vietnamese medical practice. Support Vietnamese medical colleagues and work within their supply channels. "You are not there to reform or change things," I was told. "Don't try to take over. You're there to win the hearts and minds of the people to their government… *their* government, not ours. Our Vietnamese colleagues represent that government." This was essentially and officially a *political/ military* mission, its humanitarian component secondary, not the reverse. On the other hand, my Hippocratic Oath as a physician enjoined me "above all else" to *do no harm,* while the reality on the ground, the reality that blindsided me on my arrival, was that customary Vietnamese practice was causing harm, egregious harm. Some deaths were preventable and we, the military doctors who'd volunteered for this mission, knew how to prevent them. Our orders prevented us. The irony was that our military classification as officers for this Military Provincial Hospital Augmentation Program, MILPHAP, was that of "*Preventive* Medicine" Specialist. That was my MOS (Military Occupational Specialty) and that was my ethical bind.

So, what should be my priority, my military orders or my Hippocratic Oath?

I had to choose, I could not serve both. Naturally, there were consequences to choosing either. If I didn't obey orders… I'm an officer; what did that make me? If I did obey those orders… I'm a doctor; what did *that* make me?

Complicating this conundrum, there would be no one to advise me. Not only had there been no heads-up, but there would also be no supervision or guidance. I – actually all MILPHAP doctors getting underway since 1965 – were on our own.

This much was obvious. Whatever choice I made, whatever hat I chose to wear, whatever ethical principle I placed first, I'd be betraying another. And, to add salt to this wound, there'd be no one to share the damage, pain, or blame except, of course, the two other doctors on my 15-man team. I chose my Hippocratic Oath to serve and obey.

CHAPTER 3

INTEGRITY IS MY SHOCK ORGAN THAT TAKES THE HIT

*Self-confidence, self-worth, honor, and character
all become collateral damage*

Following my betrayal, my integrity promptly became bruised, compromised, and corrupted, along with my self-confidence and self-esteem. Moral integrity, after all, means consistency in the application of the virtues and principles one embraces.

My initial reaction to this bind, before I'd made my choice, was to take refuge in the role of stranger/newcomer and concentrate on being polite, smiling, observing, and keeping my mouth shut. This, however, made things worse. It meant I was now betraying two principles instead of one. My bind was clearly a *double* bind in that I couldn't walk away, and go AWOL (Absent Without Leave). I *had* to choose. As Sancho Panza laments in the 1964 musical, *Man of La Mancha*, "Whether the stone hits the pitcher or the pitcher hits the stone, either way, it's bad for the pitcher." I was the pitcher.

The following excerpts from my diary are the sort of incidents that supported my choice of Military Orders for betrayal, not my Hippocratic Oath.

I'm assigned the Outpatient Pavilion. Patients step onto the porch and register at a booth and then enter a large room. Two Vietnamese women sit at a desk, one a civilian doctor, the other a nurse practitioner equivalent. I'm at a desk at the far end with one of my team's medics and an interpreter. It is awkward, sitting in that room with those women who don't look at me, talk to me, or return my greetings. They see all the cases. They see complicated and difficult cases and don't invite me to take a look or see if I might be of help. I can't help but wonder why. We've all been introduced at a friendly, congenial, general staff meeting wherein our role had been explained by the Vietnamese Medical Director. Is this about power, territory, or gender? Is it a cultural thing? An initiation rite? I eventually figure it out; it is none of these. It is about incompetence. Those women didn't know what they were doing and didn't care. So what is my priority? Is it still earning their trust and bonding by maintaining my passivity at the expense of patients' well-being? Or is it becoming active and interceding and seeing to it that the sick are promptly and effectively treated... thus spoiling any collegial relationship? There is no communication between us. There is no teaching. They are disinterested. So I sit, ignored, idle, polite, and waiting, as patients are ineffectively treated. And mistreated.

An infant at the Inpatient Pavilion has a fever of 105 degrees. It is customary Vietnamese practice to give such an infant an injection of a cerebral stimulant, an inappropriate, ineffective, and highly dangerous intervention. We tell our counterparts, "This won't help. Could be dangerous." "No it isn't," is the terse reply (translated). End of discussion. That practice continues.

The (American) doctor orders a medication and the hospital is out of that medication. It is customary Vietnamese practice, we learned, that when you are out of a medication you take whatever medicine you do have for that purpose and give that to the patient at the dose of the medicine you don't have. "That might cause harm," we tell our counterparts. "No it won't," is the (translated) response. End of discussion. The practice continues.

The (American) doctor orders a medication for a patient and the Vietnamese nurse assigned subsequently reports she'd dispensed it, only she hadn't. She lied. Or, the doctor orders medication for a patient and the man in charge of medicine supplies reports they are out of it. He's lying, too. It's there on the shelf. We see it. What do you do? Who do you tell? Should you even tell? What if this particular behavior is about graft, about the black market, or kickbacks? Corruption is everywhere and at all levels and everyone knows it. Our MACV superiors in Saigon know, our State Department knows, and the President knows, and it seems as if everyone over here is in on it except those being cheated, the poor in the countryside whose hearts and minds and allegiance we're charged with redirecting to the government I just described.

What do we do? Do we open up that can of worms and draw the attention of the American public to America's failures and risk being hung out to dry as whistleblowers by a vengeful White House? Or, do we get with the program, turn a blind eye, abet the corrupt system, and betray those innocent civilians who are apolitical, alienated from the Saigon government, and just want to be left in peace to till their fields and feed their families? Do we go along to get along? Orders or Oath? It wasn't long before I chose; my Physician's Oath comes first. My military mission is what I shall betray.

––––––––––––

Years passed before I let myself become cognitively aware that, in making my choice, I was indirectly prolonging the war and contributing to still more American casualties.

CHAPTER 4

INTEGRITY IS EVERYWHERE UNDER FIRE

Guilt and remorse, things we carried unseen

Was it just me, my team, or the larger MILPHAP Project taking that hit? Or, was personal integrity under fire everywhere and at all levels, top to bottom, military and civilian, over there and over here? If so, there must have been a spawning of widespread guilt and remorse compounding the baggage already weighing everyone down. It was certainly my experience, looking back.

When the war was over I did research which took my mind off myself and allowed me to get lost, as it were, in the data. I could disappear in it, inside that larger group where guilt and remorse would be distributed widely. There, I could minimize my personal guilt and remorse; maybe even bury and forget it.

That research confirmed my prediction (See Appendix I). Personal integrity was being severely beaten down everywhere. Sometimes it was totally missing; missing in action. My bonding and blaming habits, I could see, were not mine alone. The bad news was that it put me in bad company. Very bad company. So, yes, the temporary effect and the respite it offered was real. I wasn't alone. But its range and reach ended up much farther than just sorrow. It was depressing and scary.

PART II:

RECOVERY THROUGH BONDING, BLAMING, AND BLIND SPOTS

CHAPTER 5

MY SELF-RIGHTEOUS BONDING AND BLAMING

Common strategies to keep guilt and remorse at bay.
Why one part of us hates our divisiveness
while another part relies on it.

My self-righteous anger, indignation, and frustration congealed automatically around blaming someone which I eagerly indulged with like-minded colleagues. This empowered, energized, and reassured me, this self-righteous bonding and blaming. It sustained and held up my self-worth while providing a reassuring voice to my corrupted integrity. The downside, of course, was having to one day leave these like-minded colleagues and having to find others.

This experience obviously wasn't just mine. It was a part of many others' stories. Not only that, I came to suspect that human wiring must be involved given how naturally that self-righteous bonding and blaming emerged, especially given its automatic and instinctive-like features. I remembered psychological studies that pointed out that choices and decisions we make can be based on manufactured choices and decisions because, in the absence of genuine reasons, people often find one instinctively; the point being that people can instinctively search for order in the face of a baseline chaos without realizing it. In short, if we don't have it we instinctively see to it that we find it. My takeaway was simple. The pull to self-righteous bonding and blaming might be more than common and normative. It might be in our DNA.

Looking back at my wartime journal entries (samples below) gave me much to reappraise about myself. For example, (1), has to do with my post-service (civilian) habit of boasting with those I bonded with in ways that concealed my ethical failures and integrity lapses. Another, (2), does expose one ethical dilemma but buries it in American pride. Another, (3), explicitly reminds me of my instinctively reaching out to those who I knew would take my side, those who would bond with me and together with me blame others. The last, (4), does acknowledge the widening of that war but neglects any mention of my personal contribution to that catastrophe.

(1) I join the two other American doctors on my team and we make a stand. It's my first month in the country and the other two MILPHAP doctors and I have prepared our first monthly progress report for USAID (U.S. Agency for International Development headquartered in Saigon). We include in our report the observation of a customary Vietnamese practice that is egregiously inappropriate and unsafe. A complimentary copy of this report is given to the medical director of the Banmethuot government hospital who, on reading this report, is taken aback. There was a major discrepancy between what his Vietnamese doctors have been telling him and what we American doctors have just observed and are now reporting. He calls for a meeting of all doctors for an explanation of this discrepancy. Our Vietnamese counterparts speak first and say that the Americans were mistaken. What we'd reported never occurred. We then show the evidence and the Vietnamese doctors are forced to play their remaining card, the face-saving card, "Doctors shouldn't criticize other doctors." Our response, "If doctors can't criticize other doctors, who can?" falls flat.

It seems here that we've run up against an old and venerable Vietnamese tradition whereby doctors are accorded the status of Mandarin making them above criticism and beyond reproach. Vietnamese doctors function, in other words, without oversight or supervision. The Vietnamese Confucian system, we are surprised to discover, doesn't compute Western concepts of accountability and transparency. As a result, nothing is resolved, the meeting ends, our relationships with our counterparts is in shock, and we don't care. We did what was right. We told the truth.

Looking back: That confrontation became a memory that I proudly shared with colleagues and supporters at home while unconsciously obscuring the destructive impact my behavior had on our government's mission.

(2) I convert an opportunity to make amends and get our mission back on track into an opportunity for showing off. I am called to the outpatient pavilion by one of our USAID-employed interpreters before the clinic opens. It seems an unconscious youth had just been carried into the Outpatient Pavilion and placed on my examination table. My interpreter and I go promptly to the clinic where I find a small crowd standing by my examining table watching the unconscious youth who is lying supine. (They'd followed the youth's uncle when he carried his nephew there. They

wanted to see what was happening and what would happen next.) I learn the boy and his uncle had been arguing. The uncle, who had been very angry, feared the youth took an overdose. He doesn't know of what or where his nephew might have obtained drugs. While I'm listening and all eyes are on exchanges between the uncle and my interpreter, I'm watching the boy. I see his eyelids flutter. Unconscious eyes don't flutter; this boy is faking. Here is an excellent opportunity to redeem myself from the earlier confrontation over our progress report. I can refer this case to my Vietnamese colleagues (in contrast to the them-to-us referrals) and, in this way, affirm our confidence in them and because the boy is malingering I can endorse whatever treatment they proffer; it is certain to be harmless. That might help make amends and maybe restore my relationship with my counterparts to its former passive, and ostensibly benign, indifference.

I don't refer this case to the Vietnamese doctor; I keep it. I am aware there is negligible appreciation for psychological issues in Vietnamese medical training and certainly none in this rural Central Highlands culture where Western practice takes a back seat to something called "Chinese medicine" with its suction cups and acupuncture among ethnic Vietnamese living here while, for Montagnards, the tribesmen – the Central Highlands is their domain – the default treatment is animal sacrifice with ceremonies, homemade wine, and prayers. I begin by taking control of the drama (and this audience) with an alternative drama. I pick up my percussion hammer and carefully, deliberately – ceremoniously, actually – test all youth's deep tendon reflexes with frowns and murmurs to myself as I tap his ankle, knee, elbow, and wrist joints over and over, suggesting in this way that the boy's condition is serious. I conclude these absolutely unrelated and unnecessary tests with a slight nod as if in satisfaction, and put my hammer down. For this population, what I've been doing is likely to be viewed as treatment. I step back and instruct my interpreter to explain to the boy's uncle in a voice everyone can hear, especially the boy, that the boy is now OK. He's to explain that the boy will recover fully but it will begin gradually. I tell them it will begin in about 20 minutes. I step back and wait as does the small crowd. After about ten minutes the boy opens his eyes and, acting groggy begins to get up at which point he is immediately embraced by his tearful, apologetic uncle. They leave arm in arm.

Looking back: I gave no thought to the damage to my relationship with my counterparts and, through that, my mission. I gave no thought to the implications of my making my counterparts look bad as well as feel bad.

By making Americans look good, I did what I had been explicitly directed not to do. I insured that Americans wouldn't be leaving Vietnam anytime soon.

(3) It's a matter of time before someone up the chain-of-command notices and I draw a reprimand but I'm now seeing patients regularly and have begun to observe, in young Montagnard girls coming to the Outpatient Pavilion, an unsightly skin condition affecting much of their body. This is serious because that rash renders these girls un-marriageable and, in a society like theirs, living close to the land, one's having daughters who do not bring men or sons into the family, is consequential.

The French called this skin condition scabies. Americans and Vietnamese call it scabies, too, and there is plenty of scabies cream at the hospital but that cream doesn't help. I investigate and find out why. It isn't scabies. It isn't caused by a tiny arthropod, a mite. It's a fungus and this fungus doesn't respond to cream on the skin. It only responds to a medication taken internally, a pill that does not exist in the Vietnamese supply system.

We'd been directed not to reach outside the Vietnamese supply channels for supplies but I write home anyway to colleagues and friends and ask them to send me samples of Griseofulvin. That's the medicine. I use it, it works, the skin condition is cured and the girls are thrilled and their families relieved and I'm in trouble. I am reprimanded by superiors at MACV Headquarters in Saigon who repeat that we are not to use medications that come outside regular Vietnamese supply channels. "Even if it's life or death?" I challenge. "Even if it's life or death! Remember why we're here! We're here to win the hearts and minds of the people to their government; theirs, not ours!" A visiting congressman to whom I'd explained the problem, solution, and outcome, and who'd expressed admiration and support for what I'd done subsequently wrote and retracted his approval. He asked that I stop.

Looking back: Like other MILPHAP doctors in-country, I had been writing home asking for supplies. Families who had been sending those supplies had begun writing their congressmen to ask why their sons weren't given the supplies they needed to do their jobs. The government resolved this matter, not by explaining that the primary objective of our mission was political and military and not humanitarian, but by directing that the doctors stop asking for outside help. Naturally, when I told this story to my selective audiences, I was always the hero. I never spoke of my experience from the strategic perspective – my Military Orders and mission. I kept buried, from myself as well as others, the reality that by helping prolong the war, I was also a villain.

(4) Eventually my disregard for military orders takes a fragile turn. This occurs when I demonstrate publicly that we Americans are ready and willing to step in, pick up the slack, and do what the Vietnamese can but don't do for themselves. One day, following a similar episode by the MILPHAP doctor assigned to the In-Patient Pavilion, I ask my medics to collect all the mops, pails, and Borax they can commandeer and we proceed to wash down our area, our examining tables, etc. It is following this bold and heady initiative that I manifestly disobey orders. My Vietnamese physician counterpart has routinely been sending new patients for injections and pills without even a pretense of asking questions or an examination and I have not intervened, content to see only those patients they allow to see me, but today is different. Today, it is a sick child in her mother's arms who is given this fast-lane treatment and this was my tipping point. I chase the mother down as she walks away with the piece of paper with "treatment" instructions and I bring her and her child back to my examining table, take a history, examine the child, make my diagnosis and order the effective treatment and write it all down. I take and discard the note my counterpart had given the mother and replace it with my own and send her for my recommended treatment. Then I sit down; I need to calm myself. I am agitated and angry. The next day a crowd of sick people appear, both Vietnamese and Montagnard, outside the outpatient pavilion asking to see the American doctor.

On the one hand, there had been a boost in morale of non-medical hospital staff following those scrub downs. Also, the reputation of the hospital, following my outburst and attention to that child had, it seemed, earned a measure of trust among many people. On the other hand, I had egregiously embarrassed and alienated my Vietnamese medical colleagues, pulling the rug out from under any likelihood of repair of our relationship, and I'd performed the ultimate act of sabotage of my mission, showing for all to see our American willingness to jump in, take over, fix things, and fix them right. The unpopular Saigon government, already sinking under the burden of its image and reputation as an American "puppet," now sinks even deeper into illegitimacy along with their dependence on America, following behaviors such as mine. This was 1965.

Looking back: The war was now formally our American War, and the numbers of American casualties were beginning to seriously climb, and still, I'd given no thought to my role in this back then.

When I learned later about the MILPHAP team that had been kicked out by their Vietnamese Medical Director of the Province that they'd been assigned to, and then about the MILPHAP doctor who'd had a mental breakdown and had to return home, I couldn't help but wonder if those events and my conundrum, my issues of ethics and betrayal, weren't related. Now, I can't help but view my blaming propensity back then as linked to our current epidemic of blaming. Back then, of course, it was a combination of our military directing the blame at politicians, politicians directing blame at the press and emerging anti-war protestors, anti-war protesters directing blame at combat soldiers, and combat soldiers directing blame at anti-war protesters, and everyone blaming Secretary of Defense, Robert McNamara, and President Johnson. It's only now, years later, in the context of our toxic divisiveness, that self-righteous bonding and blaming smells like the same homemade device used years before to drown out something coming from inside us. If it is, our participation in today's divisiveness may be tied to a lurking awareness like before, that if we were to stop barking at someone else, something inside us would be barking at us. Perhaps bonding and blaming have not just been our diversion. Perhaps it has also been our shield.

It was with that in mind that I wondered how many G.I.s took home an experience of bonding and self-righteous blaming like me, not just over shared danger and shared relief, but also, like with me, over shared guilt along with confusion and anger. I wondered about this because I'd noticed that now, years later, when veterans are told they are heroes, they not uncommonly cringe. Was this because real heroes might see their deception, the real heroes being those who performed brave deeds for a noble cause, not those who, like them, would rather not remember their small betrayals and all the other misdeeds in their past that get resurrected by such a tease? Was it that they didn't want to be reminded of past regrets and compromises, and certainly didn't want to be derailed by self-recrimination or remorse that perpetually lay in wait? (When I became aware that there are roughly twenty veteran suicides daily, I began finding it very hard to drop this bone.)

A part of me wants to assure those veterans, all veterans, that they may be called heroes simply because people need heroes to let *their* sleeping dogs lie. People, for example, who'd avoided service, and those who'd scorned and derided returning soldiers those many years ago, even those who never faced a military draft and now those post-draft who never enlisted and want to keep it that way, are now grateful for volunteers. They all might even need a symbolic "atonement" for those personal shortcomings. Applauding a man or woman in uniform might not just represent a need for heroes. It might also represent a gesture of honor for those who never made it back. In short, it might be a balm for all manner of unhealed wounds.

I wish I could tell those veterans not to take the public honor personally but accept it graciously. It might not be about what they did or even what they stand for, or even them. It might simply represent what the crowd needs, namely a channel to affirm and exercise their better nature. Vets don't have to cringe. The service you're performing *now* is your honorable service. In short, you are here giving voice to and honor for that crowd's better nature.

Looking back, it's as if we Americans have drifted seamlessly into a comfort zone that, despite being a dark valley, seduces us into remaining here by promising that sleeping dogs in our heads will continue to lie (pun not intended) and wouldn't wake here anyway. Here, in this foul air, there is no shortage of foes against us and no shortage of like-minded to bond with. We may be breathing foul air and unable to see clear skies, but we can't help but feel invigorated, alert, and full of ourselves here in this exciting valley of toxic discourse.

Looking back, because there is no shortage of targets for us to blame we can fill our mental lives with blaming. Is it the silence, then, that we fear? Is it that a quietness might waken our sleeping dogs? Is all our white noise of annoyance and frustration actually a diversion that lets our sleeping dogs lie? If so, then while a part of us hates our divisiveness, another part may be relying on it; that while we bark at one another, our sleeping dogs inside us don't bark at us. At any rate, it feels that way to me. When they aren't barking at me, my self-esteem and self-confidence remain safe. So, if that part of me is that fragile, I really do have a job ahead. To save another's world I best continue to open myself up more to my Self.

CHAPTER 6

OUR VIRTUOUS BLIND SPOT:
OUT OF SIGHT, OUT OF MIND

It was my political leaders
who showed me how to live with corruption successfully and honorably,
but not how to process and deal with it.

Midrash on Genesis 38, Looking Without Seeing

Judah, son of Jacob, after convincing his brothers to sell their youngest brother, Joseph, into slavery and then, together with those brothers, lying to their father by claiming the lad was dead, rendered their father forever heartbroken and held at arm's length from them. We read that compounding these dishonorable actions is Judah's subsequent neglectful behavior towards his daughter-in-law Tamar, thus keeping her legally tied to his surviving son, Shelah, without allowing her to actually marry him. His is a less than upstanding life. However, his outward presentation to others tells them that his way is the way of righteousness. This is a mask, of course. While we may expect on some level that he might actually be troubled by his past offenses and lapses, the biblical text infers otherwise, namely that he gives no thought to those failings; that he has successfully blocked them out of the picture. He doesn't see what's behind his own mask. For Judah his mask is him. In other words, his image of who he is is incomplete, which, interestingly, is mirrored in the image he has of the prostitute he recently had sex with and who he has now sentenced to death. The image he has of her is also incomplete. It turns out she, too, is hiding behind a mask, the difference being hers is conscious and deliberate and facing outward; his faces outward *and* inward and is neither deliberate nor conscious. The prostitute is Judah's daughter-in-law, Tamar, and she has an agenda. Judah's facile readiness to pass deadly judgment on her, the ultimate price, in the face of his obliviousness to the price he is not paying for his moral lapses, reveals not just how low he has fallen but how unlikely will be any recovery, any reform or redemption, any recognition on his part, let alone owning to and then integrating, his own missing pieces, all necessary for him to become whole again. And healed.

My 21st Century Midrash Takeaway

Recovery, reform, and redemption from one's past misdeeds are unlikely to happen without some illumination of one's blind spots. First, we need to begin seeing something that we may have been looking at but not seeing. We need to begin integrating our "missing pieces" to complete our Selves. In short, we need to open up, accept, and process more of who we are. Not surprisingly, the process of becoming more whole is considered a process of becoming more healed. Currently, we're in the process of coming apart, individually and as a whole.

Once I'd made my choice to obey my medical oath and disobey military orders and their objective, if I ever had occasion to look again at those orders and that objective and the consequences of my choice, I never saw them. They had become as if out of my sight and, for me, out of sight meant out of mind.

It had all entered what I call my blind spot. I never gave thought, for example, to the fact that my undermining the image and authority of the Vietnamese health system would directly contribute to the delay of the Saigon government gaining the support and legitimacy it needed for victory. This never made it onto my radar. The fact that my demonstration of America's readiness, even eagerness, to pick up the slack for Vietnamese counterparts, would contribute to the prolongation of our American presence there, never made it onto my radar, either. Such behaviors of mine, reinforcing the image of the Saigon government as an American "puppet" and thus illegitimate and unworthy of their citizens' loyalty, only contributed to the prolonging of the war with continued American casualties. I gave no thought to any of this. My role as a malignant facilitator was off my radar and I did not see what I was becoming.

All this "denial" occurred without deliberate effort or conscious desire. It just happened, automatically, reflexively, and defensively. It was this instinctive defensive purpose that had led me to consider that it might be part of my wiring – part of *our* wiring – a DNA survival asset. Consistent with that, of course, was not having memories of fretting or wringing my hands, obsessing and doubting myself, or becoming indecisive once I'd made my choice. I remembered only a seamless entry into bonding and blaming, courtesy of this blind spot bonus.

Guilt and remorse, of course, can prove deadly and wear a person down.

It can make living intolerable, unbearable, unsustainable, and invite death. But, a reflex burial of an experience into a blind spot does buy time. One does need to wait until ready to rally and deal with a difficult and problematic decision while we, in the meantime, keep going. Once again, it feels like a survival thing.

In my quest for the truth and my need for peace of mind, I made a list of some of the major decisions by our leaders in the context of *their* ethical binds. (See Appendix II) This quickly confirmed for me that they too had operational blind spots. I wasn't alone in my betrayals. In fact, I was in good company. And, like with me, it seemed that much of what was buried inside our leaders' blind spots could best be viewed as variations of disrespect for the humanity of others. My gathered information about them and the contexts of their decisions did, nonetheless, bring me a measure of peace of mind. It was certainly a successful diversion for me. However, it ended up prompting yet more questions and speculations about connections between what happened back then and what was happening now. If, for example, a main motivation for our leaders back then, tuning out and burying realities and memories, was less about our nation than about their personal honor, self-image, and future, then the toxicity in our civil discourse today is like them back then. There's a connection that presents as a continuation.

Like those leaders back then, it's the bright side of things that fills space in our minds. The so-called blind spots are, of course, unknown. The point is we are spared regret, remorse, and simple acknowledgment of harm done by us. The downside to that is, of course, a weakening of our self-respect and, with it, our sense of integrity. It's here I began wondering if the reason we avoid displays of humility and respect for the humanity of others is to stay clear of showing signs of weakness because those behaviors are linked to weakness. But, weakness, I began realizing, was already there. Those acts of humility simply exposed it. It's easy to confuse the two.

That was when I realized that the fear of appearing weak or just feeling weak, signified I wasn't being fully open to myself. It signified that I was not fully "there." It pointed out that my becoming more "there" about myself would be becoming more "there" in myself. And becoming more "there" was becoming more fully my Self. Here I felt I was getting closer to a "saving a world" step.

In the meantime, and from those reports (Appendix II), I found confirmation that there was a link between the divisive discourse in the Vietnam War era and today's discourse. It came as I was recalling the moment in 1973 when we withdrew from Vietnam dishonorably and were told it was honorable. We were all told we'd accomplished our goal and, with that spin, everyone, at last, was feeling relief – the hawks and doves both. The hemorrhaging had stopped and both sides had reason to celebrate and were eager to move on but, resolving differences and then moving on is not the same thing as simply moving on. We simply moved on. What followed, I've come to believe, was a slow-motion catching up, for both our now evolved groupings and our very private Selves. The catching up was achieved and succeeded by our keeping a lid on our buried, under-the-radar, uneasiness, and insecurities. I began suspecting that those had been handed down somehow through the generations. Maybe it was handed down in the form of shifting attitudes and interesting behaviors accompanied by fresh values and new habits.

PART III:

TODAY'S TOXIC VALLEY:
I'D BEEN PREPPED

CHAPTER 7

OBSERVATIONS FROM INSIDE
MY COLD-COMFORT ZONE

Americans don't give up, give in, or submit.
A sign of both toughness and fragility.

My practice in bonding and blaming, supported by my blind spot, not only allowed me to continue my life with no remorse over misdeeds of the past, but also shielded me from becoming too caught up in the consequences of increasingly divisive discourse. I'd been prepped, you might say. That shield, however, obliged me to keep feeding the current divisiveness, now – I'm embarrassed to say – my comfort zone. Here, I join in and "play that card" just like everybody else, only now I know I'm not only contributing to an ongoing toxic stalemate, I'm contributing to the increase in its toxicity. It keeps worsening. Cold comfort.

Looking about me now, I could see that it was as if all of America had resigned itself to a repetition of former generations' interminable stalemates experienced in the Cold and Vietnam Wars where one side, our side, had to win and the other would just have to give up, give in, and submit. The difference, of course, is that this time the enemy is a fellow American and so we are all, ourselves, enemies of fellow Americans. In any case, either case, and each case, we seem to have forgotten that Americans don't give up, give in, or submit; meaning, we're in this forever. But, inasmuch as I was now in the process of trying, at least symbolically, to find a way to break free of the more hurtful and painful side to this stand-off, the toxicity to this national affliction and conundrum, I had to focus on figuring out what I must *not* do. That meant looking carefully inside me as well as around me.

This is what I saw. This current comfort zone of stalemate has been transmitted now through several generations. Even in the time of Covid, teens, like their parents, have not only comfortably adapted to easing behavior constraints and expectations, but also comfortably adopted the language of superlatives, exaggerations, and other signals so that hype is now our popular coin of social exchange. Like everyone else I, too, became comfortable with this exaggerated jargon. Someone's debatable decision was "total disaster!" I, too, was no longer surprised when a friend presenting an opposing view would be dismissed by others as an "absolute traitor." And I couldn't help but notice that social hurt now entitled one to "victim" status and I was becoming comfortable with "GREAT" and "WOW" replacing "good" and "fine." Given the universality and intensity of hype, I had to once again wonder; were we in denial of an underlying fragility? The flip side of pumped-up is, after all, deflation.

Those observations of our preference for superlatives and our attachment to hype made me wonder whether the comfort and eagerness to grab hold of such a handle signaled that one now had a purpose. My guess was that such a purpose surely included recognition and hope. Those superlatives were as if messengers. They certainly gave users like me a boost. For example, nowadays, respectful acknowledgment of another's point of view is tantamount to an admission that one's own point of view is likely tentative, perhaps even insecure. That, of course, rocks the boat. It rocks mine. When I acknowledge another's point of view as potentially interesting and worth considering, it often leaves me feeling more vulnerable and exposed, than respectful. In short, it doesn't seem we have much tolerance for weakness nowadays. Defensiveness seems to have become more like a default posture than a contribution to genuine discourse.

In my conversations with myself on these developments, one example always comes to mind. When North Korea pushes for nuclear capability with an inter-continental missile, America almost routinely feels obliged to focus on how to intimidate them into submission and make them let go of that plan and back away from that goal. We appear to have no interest in getting into that leader's head. But getting into his head and seeing what's there and why – his motivation – appears the obvious and critical path. So putting our minds at ease always seems more important than examining an enemy's mind's un-ease. Part of me is thinking: what if he's telling the truth when he says it's for defense? What if his concern about being threatened isn't about the sort of attack we envision? He's a human being, after all, like us, and neither "Evil" nor a "Monster." What if his defense isn't against an assault on his life, his territory, or his people? What if it's an assault on his integrity? What if the threat is his loss of face with shame? What if it's not about death but dishonor? The code that places death before dishonor, after all, isn't exclusive to the West, And, what if it's a defense against an assault not about to erupt but one that erupted long ago and is ongoing and has yet to let up? What should be one's strategy for dealing with this? Wouldn't talks that highlight listening be a familiar, effective, safe, and honorable place to start? Inserting missiles in South Korea and conducting military exercises in nearby waters, in this context, would be dramatically and frighteningly counter-productive. Shouldn't our leaders lead us sometimes, not just follow us? (If we say our President wanting to hear the other side is a sign of weakness, it's *our* weakness talking, not the President's. Let's not forget that.) Which brings me back to my query; what am I *not* to do here? How do I get myself out of the way of healing?

In America here and now, I find myself thinking, neither side – almost none of us – is comfortable debating or respectfully discussing our differences with the other side. Few people I know are thinking of getting close enough to understand and, maybe, respect another's motive. This time, I'm thinking, it's no longer a fear of being labeled "soft on communism" or "traitor" as in bygone years, losing our jobs, and ruining our careers. Or, simply feeling guilty as in other wars. This time, I'm beginning to realize, it's because the push-back, commotion, and bad feelings that always erupt, will come, not from politicians, employers, or strangers, but from colleagues and friends. They'll come from our children, our brothers and sisters, our husbands and wives, and our family. They'll come from our own conscience and we're really not ready to go there. It doesn't feel safe enough. So, we preach to the choir, to like-minded colleagues. Or, we preach at non-choir members from a distance, knowing we can hang up that phone, as it were, turn off the TV, put down the newspaper, or hit a "delete" button. (Unless, of course, we're into dust-ups, put-downs, uproar; or into acting out our anger and blame, in which case it helps to have so many proxies on which to unload and unwind. Proxies, it turns out, are everywhere and available. And it's all so exciting and makes for such popular reading, and highlights so many exciting news stories.)

Absent respectful talks with my foes, my customary mindset continues to be cautiously defensive. Ironically, it serves to contain and restrain me not unlike a strait-jacket, except that the posture of arms-crossed signals determination here, not powerlessness. As a strategy, I've found this posture satisfying. It embodies just the right spirit, the self-righteous, defensive spirit I've become used to. But applied out of context it can exude a toxic nastiness. "Bend but don't break" has probably by now morphed into, "Never bend. Make the other guy break." The example that quickly comes to mind is: You're driving a one-lane road and the car in front suddenly and inexplicably slows to a crawl. What comes to mind is no longer, "Oh! Is he lost? In trouble?" but something more akin to, "Damn! Can you believe that jerk!" That's the self-righteous spirit taking charge in the wheelhouse of the mind. Why else, I ask myself, when someone says, "Thank you," for something one did, our response is no longer a gracious, "You're welcome" but rather, "No problem" which implies we're not at all put-off, or offended by doing what we just did for you. It's as if even default relationships must be viewed as adversarial.

How seamlessly this adversarial posture, "Us versus Them," "Me versus not Me," begs the same question. I'm thinking here, not just of the likes of road rage, but of the allure of the ideologue offering a path to heroic martyrdom. I'm thinking of the easy submission to the demagogue who incites anger and blame, promising relief with redemption. Arguably, the many faces of political correctness where honest differences become intolerable deviations from orthodoxy, as well as those egregious failures of self-restraint such as hate speech, all belong here. Or, the popular iterations of indignant victimhood whereby one gains traction and advantage from one's bruised integrity and incomplete Self rather than seeks repair. It's increasingly obvious to me now that we Americans may be Number One in many areas but, in this valley, listening isn't one of them. Pondering one obvious question that seems to follow such incidents, encounters, and behaviors – "What were they thinking!" I think I already know the answer. They weren't thinking, they were reacting. They weren't responding to a thought that registered in their minds. They were responding to a feeling that they felt in their guts. The two are different. It's so important to keep that in mind.

CHAPTER 8

ONE LIGHT THAT FAILED: OUR AMERICAN STORY

Our mantra is "We're Number One," our by-word, "Can Do."
So, why haven't we resolved this toxicity problem?
(And why do I feel smaller?)

I've known that many nations have their national story and understand that their narrative explains how life – individual and national – is a work in progress, and cautions that there are bumps in the road and detours. I've known that those stories imply that there is always more to come, always more expected and more to be done, meaning there is always a future. Worldwide, it seems, such stories, some designated sacred, keep people vital and whole in the face of life's slings and arrows. I've also long been aware and appreciated that those stories represent goals to strive for as well as protective shields that sustain us in hard times. But, narrative shields, like so much else in life, do have their seasons. Applied at the wrong time or for the wrong reason, shields can fail to protect. Worse, they can get in the way. In fact, they *have* gotten in our way. They are *still* in our way.

It was time for me to give our national story, our American Story, another look. It was, after all, the essence of who we were and who we are, and who we were and are is Number One. At least that's been its most popular sound bite. It's the keeper of our exceptional status and destiny, our source of pride, confidence, and inspiration. It's also our narrative shield, having been a reliable source of safety, protection, and reassurance when threatened. My second look, however, pointed something out that I'd missed. Inasmuch as our lived reality has a way of periodically thrusting vulnerability in our face, and given that this shield is myth-based as well as evidence-based, I now see more clearly why we naturally, intuitively, and repeatedly omit a qualifier to our being Number One. There can be no challenge if this is to have its desired effect.

The wisdom behind remaining quiet about just what it is that we're Number One in becomes apparent. It has been for reassurance. I hadn't realized that Number One also functioned as a mask. Of course, concealing our insecurity behind that mask rather than reflecting it, ensures uninterrupted peace of mind. Why else would we conspicuously avoid noticing that our foreign neighbors can rightfully complain that they are rendered less worthy by our Number One claim? It was as if such sensitivity to how others must feel in the face of our boastings might signify weakness on our part, and appearing soft and weak to others would mean to us, vulnerability. So, of course, concealing and boasting tops explaining and understanding.

As I came to view it, the more we applied this boast of exceptionalism as a mask to conceal our insecurity, the more we'd experience our myth-infused identity as reality. And the more we experienced it as reality, the less it became a goal to pursue or a beacon to guide us. The two had conflated long ago because we were already there. The two were now interchangeable. No surprise, then, that the more I looked at myself the less I saw. I was becoming more and more incomplete, like everyone else. That meant, in terms of our nation, there was now little genuine reflection and certainly no recalculation. In place of reflection and recalculation was our being seduced into revisiting and remembering only our good deeds. We'd been oriented to the perspective that American generosity has been too often unappreciated or forgotten. Those moments of defensively rallying 'round our flag had been essentially our defensively shoring up that shield. I could see that the focus had to be, not only on us not seeing them, but on them not seeing us. It was certainly about us not seeing ourselves.

The Vietnam experience comes to mind again. Our European friends thought we were crazy to remain there but that never translated to a national discussion or debate that I recall. Instead, we bravely declared, and proudly, that we'd stand tall and go it alone if we must. It felt like a moral crusade. We were fighting Evil. I still remember that WW II poster of a determined Uncle Sam rolling up his sleeves as the going got tough. That was the image we American's always wanted to embody and project, the message we needed to send. It's easier now to see why I became soured. It's all in our "Can Do!" sound bite. I could see how, when we Americans proudly think and declare, without qualification, "Can Do!," I could also see that this declaration, this powerful and successful motivator and well-earned affirmation of what we've accomplished, can also backfire. When applied at the wrong time or in the wrong place, or over the wrong deed, it does backfire. I checked and found an example. I found it in General Bruce Palmer, Jr.'s explanation of why the Joint Chiefs of Staff (JCS) didn't address the impossibility of their troops engaging the enemy in battle frequently enough to win our war of attrition. As he explained it, it was because the JCS "were imbued with the 'can do' spirit and could not bring themselves to make… a negative statement or to appear to be disloyal."[3] Looking back, wouldn't the strategic thing have been to say, No, this cannot be done. Not now. Let's recalculate?

Still more began falling into place for me. Reflecting on our ambitious nation-building objective in Vietnam in the 1950s and our intention to make the world safe, I could see that we never adjusted and course-corrected as needed, based on recalculations. I could see now with more clarity how we, instead, allowed that mission to quietly morph into one of defeat avoidance. We were playing catchup because an obstacle had been placed in our path and was forcing us to swerve and detour. At last, I could see more clearly how our narrative shield that so gallantly lets us in had let us down. For me, this impression was confirmed when, in my reading, I read where McNamara noted with chagrin as he listed the reasons for our failure in Vietnam: "We failed to recognize that in international affairs, as in other aspects of life, there may be problems for which there are no immediate solutions. For one whose life had been dedicated to the belief and practice of problem-solving, this is particularly hard to admit. But, at times, we may have to live with an imperfect, untidy world."[4] In a word (or two), for me, McNamara was saying that there comes a time for us to say, "Can't" do.

So, back to the present, ours now is a nation, torn by a fissure, and stuck in a miserable standoff. Fighting and winning on foreign soil is now totally out of reach. Our American Story is of no help and self-paralysis is pretty well fixed as today's mode. I can't help, of course, having the residual gut feelings of anger at an American Story that has repeatedly let us down by declining sensible, albeit untidy, compromises. I fault that American Story for its gallant – if impossible – dream, that introduced the stream of ethical compromises with betrayals and corrupted integrities that spawned my blind spots and self-righteous blaming. What I've only recently begun to understand is how it so smoothly blended in with American lives two generations later with a similar divisive civil discourse that has, again, entrenched the two groups, only now leaving us paralyzed, albeit safe enough.

Our bonding and blaming with support from our blind spots has entered a new phase; this toxic phase where being safe has morphed to, "safe enough."

---

3. General Bruce Palmer, Jr., *Twenty-five Year War: America's Military Role in Vietnam* (Lexington, KY: University Press of Kentucky, 1984), p. 46.

4. Robert S. McNamara, *In Retrospect: The Tragedy and Lessons of Vietnam* (New York: Times Books, 1995), p. 323.

PART IV:

SAVE ANOTHER'S LIFE,
SAVE ANOTHER'S WORLD –
GATHERING DATA

CHAPTER 9

GETTING OUT OF THE WAY OF HEALING:
THE ROLE OF RELATIONSHIPS AND WORDS
IN BECOMING WHOLE

*The concept of getting out of the way of healing
is neither unknown nor new.*

Midrash on Babylonian Talmud Berakhot 5b,[5] Clinging to Suffering

This offers insight into why we sometimes appear to cling to suffering and how that behavior interferes with healing. The text:

Rabbi Chiyya bar Abba became ill.
Rabbi Yochanan came to see him. He said to him: Is your suffering pleasing to you?
He said to him: Neither it nor its reward.
He said to him: Give me your hand.
He gave him his hand, and he lifted him up.

Rabbi Yochanan became ill.
Rabbi Chanina came to see him. He said to him: Is your suffering pleasing to you?
He said to him: Neither it nor its reward.
He said to him: Give me your hand.
He gave him his hand and he lifted him up.

Why? So that Rabbi Yochanan should lift himself up?
It is said: "The prisoner cannot free himself from prison."

Rabbi Elazar became sick.
Rabbi Yochanan came to see him.

5. Rabbi William Cutter, PhD, Editor, *Midrash & Medicine: Healing Body and Soul in the Jewish Interpretive Tradition*, (Vermont: Jewish Lights Publishing, 2011), pp. 107–108.

He saw that he was lying in a dark place. Rabbi Yochanan uncovered his arm and light fell from it.

He saw that Rabbi Elazar was crying.

He said to him: Why are you crying? If you are crying because you did not accomplish enough Torah, surely we have learned: it makes no difference whether you accomplish a great deal of Torah or a small amount, as long as your heart is directed toward heaven.

Or if it is because you had little money to sustain yourself – not every man earns two tables.

If it is because you didn't have a lot of children or any, in fact, see, here is the bone of my tenth son.

He said to him: I am crying on account of this beauty that will waste in the dust.

He said to him: Surely that is what you are crying for.

So the two of them cried.

Either way he said to him: Is your suffering pleasing to you?

He said to him: Neither it nor its reward.

He said to him: Give me your hand.

He gave him his hand and lifted him up.

What is going on here? This text begins simply and unremarkably enough. "Rabbi Chiyya bar Abba became ill and a Rabbi Yochanan came to see him." Then, abruptly, the narrative becomes terse and cryptic. "He said to him: Is your suffering pleasing to you? He said to him: Neither it nor its reward. He said to him: Give me your hand. He gave him his hand, and he lifted him up." Whoa! Slow down! Say again?

Slowed down it seems that this text is like shorthand, and those phrases are sound bites, and their meaning has no mystery. "Is your suffering pleasing to you?" is a variant of the familiar, "You're wallowing in self-pity. Happy now?" Of course, we don't see this because we aren't expecting something so sarcastic, provocative, and confrontational from rabbis who are scholars and colleagues, especially rabbis who are friends. But this seems precisely what it is, a chiding, and it is, indeed, personal. Only it is not a rebuke. It is a slap-in-the-face wake-up call. Those of us who were witnesses to the Vietnam War are reminded of the scene in the 1968 Mel Brooks movie, *The Producers*, where Zero Mostel's Max Bialystok slaps the face of Gene Wilder's distraught and hysterical, out-of-control Leo Bloom, following which Bloom immediately pulls himself together declaring, "Thanks, I needed that!"

Most everyone back then, the War, the Silent, and the Boomer Generations (along with, it appears, the Biblical and early Common Era Generations as well), would likely have recognized, appreciated, and smiled at such an act, moment, and outcome. (This is probably less the case in the U.S. today since battery has become criminalized.) Truth is, a slap can and does break someone out of a helpless mindset or state of denial and return him or her to a state of awareness and control. It does work. Leo Bloom's, "Thanks, I needed that!" was exclaimed, not murmured, and for good reason. Exclaiming rather than murmuring affirms that the slap accomplished its purpose, did its job and the "slapee" is back in control (with no need for another slap). Which is likely why scholars who've weighed in on that response in this text have elected to include an exclamation mark, "Neither it nor its reward!"

That verbal "slap" appears to work for Rabbi bar Abba because, in his response, bar Abba promptly volunteers the assurance that, not only has he dispensed with the "pleasure" of his wretchedness and suffering, he is no longer going to be accepting secondary-gain either from any attention he's been receiving from it, or, for that matter, any distraction his suffering might have provided him from other, more troublesome issues. "I get it!" bar Abba seems to be declaring with this trenchant riposte, "Neither it nor its reward!" (Exclamation point mine). He makes clear he's back to himself. (Of course, this declaration could have been merely out of an eagerness to put a hold on a second slap; the text is ambiguous on this point, but it doesn't matter. That prompt and energetic response wherein bar Abba is giving as good as he is getting, is confirmation enough.)

To continue, the similarities of word count between this question and answer have surely invited readers, thinking these words in their minds, to wonder how they might have sounded in their original language. Such a brisk, military cadence might well have been deliberate. Such a cadence is common in the military everywhere. Question-response, shouted – picture army recruits marching on a parade ground – generates and deepens interpersonal bonding, strengthens group cohesion, and even lifts individual spirits (recalling, too, some of the chants heard in the streets of American cities during the 1960s protests, the leaders shouting, "What do we want?" and the crowd responding, "Peace!"; then, "When do we want it?" followed by, "Now!," repeated like a mantra, building to a crescendo). It may be immaterial, in other words, whether bar Abba's response was merely to avoid a second "slap" because, at that moment of repartee, he has let go of his suffering. And, according to what comes next, it is permanent. The final lines to this cryptic account, read as a summation metaphor for what happened, only un-nuanced and behavioral, confirms this. "He said to him: Give me your hand. He gave him his hand and he lifted him up." That's it in a nutshell; that's the recap. There was a reaching out, a taking of a hand, and a lifting up of a fellow; a succinct and elegant summary. What had likely been, in reality, a profound inner transformation of a long-suffering fellow with seriously complicated issues, is here distilled to this singular take-home image, this visual rendition, this metaphor-snapshot that won't easily be forgotten.

There's more. The story is then repeated, only now Rabbi Yochanan is the one who suffers. This is followed by: "Why? So that Rabbi Yochanan should lift himself up? It is said: 'The prisoner cannot free himself from prison.'" What does this retelling tell us? It's the same story, word for word, the only difference being a reversal of roles for Yochanan, followed by that prison analogy. What it tells us is that a person can fill both roles and that both roles may be required to free oneself from one's prison.

From here we infer the following: Interpersonal relationships that enable recovery may not be simply contextual, they may be critical. There is the wake-up call, the "slap" – the voice that catalyzes – and then there is the "follow-through" voice, the "I get it" voice. And then this inference: Recovery may require two voices and one of them may be one's own. If you find yourself suffering and not believing you have control over your suffering and in need of someone to make you see that you do have control, you may have to, *yourself,* speak that other voice, to *your* self. (And, if you're like Rabbi Yochanan and have already been speaker and listener to that voice – which is probably all of us – you can do it.)

And, finally, this. These two stories are part of a trilogy, the third story following the same format as the other two with the same opening and same ending, only offering details in between. Rabbi Elazar is the one suffering now. Rabbi Yochanan is once again, the healer. This third story makes this point. The one suffering, the sick person, might not be the only one unaware that letting go of one's suffering is an option. The healer might be unaware as well, especially if that suffering person is dying. In this story Yochanan probably suspects that some of Elazar's suffering and crying might include a bit of self-indulgence, and not just because he knows him that well; Elazar was a former student. It's because he knows *himself* that well. Rabbi Yochanan has found himself in Rabbi Elazar's shoes before, so to speak. He, like Elazar, is a public figure who enjoys his good looks, his personal beauty, and vanity. Yochanan could be talking about himself here and, in a sense, he is, when he asks for reasons for Elazar's crying, and then offers as possible reasons those most "kosher" – piety and poverty – adding unnecessarily his own credentials as sufferer, as if there is a competition or blurring of boundaries. Elazar volunteers the truth, his embarrassing truth, and Yochanan sees the whole picture. Elazar's tears, it seems, are rooted neither in piety nor poverty. They are rooted in the loss of his good looks, his vanity. "I am crying," Elazar confesses, "on account of this beauty (of mine) that will waste in the dust." His suffering is, in part, a narcissistic, regressive, self-indulgence.

What happens next is both remarkable and predictable. Rabbi Elazar continues his crying of course, only now Rabbi Yochanan cries, too. They cry together. Elazar has, after all, the most justifiable of reasons for suffering, his approaching death, his light going out, and his pending return to "dust." But then, after sharing tears, Yochanan addresses that other issue, the vanity and self-pity that Elazar is still clinging to and Yochanan gets right down to business, his verbal "slap." And it works, as confirmed by the familiar chants-cum-sound-bite summary: "Is your suffering pleasing to you?" "Neither it nor its reward!" (Exclamation point mine).

Here is the final meaning of that third story: Despite our misery, even when we have the best of justifications for feeling miserable, there may still be a portion of our suffering that we cling to deliberately and unnecessarily. And, even when this portion of our suffering that we can let go, but don't, is insignificant, we should let go of it anyway simply because we can, because we are better than that and because we are more than that.

My 21st Century Midrash Takeaway

To get out of the way of my own healing, in a nutshell, is to let the rest of me come out into the open, into my awareness, because I am more than what I seem. If that means admitting to my insecurity and self-doubt, I admit to it. If it means acknowledging my uncertainty and confusion, I acknowledge it. If it opens my memory to shameful behavior, I let it open. And if in the face of any of this, I desperately need to be assured I am seen and cared for, I'll find it in the words and relationships with others if not myself. Translation: It's lowering the shields that are hiding parts of us from ourselves that gets us out of the way of healing.

In this Midrash, it was a resistance to moving beyond one's misery that got in the way of healing, something that was neither new nor unknown. Overcoming this resistance, I now see clearly, can involve simply a relationship and words. In this text, the pain and suffering represented something regressive, something immature, petty, and vain. Vanity was the obstacle. Vanity was indulged, not addressed. The poor soul was prepared to die with it as well as for it. He was prepared to take it to the grave because of a narcissistic wound, nothing to be proud of or remembered for. It might seem impossible to shake, especially facing death because, at such times, it's as if that person clinging to a private weakness and secret shame can't break free, as if that weakness and shame were clinging to him. That person is in obvious need of help in revealing this more complete self and that way allowing a private as well as public image, and honesty as well as reputation and Good Name, to be honored while facing death, not a regressed and lesser self.

As I saw it, the service the caregiver offered was, in addition to a firm respect for who his friend had once become, a relationship and words. That relationship communicated through action: "I know you, I feel for you, I'm prepared to shake and chastise you as well as cry with you. I am here, I see you, and I care." Actions do speak louder than words. Actions can declare. (Here they declared: "You may be dying physically and that can't be helped, but your Self, your spirit, your integrity as a person need not be dying in anticipation of the end, and I'm here on behalf of that integrity, too.") There was no whining, negativism, or regression, during those two-way bedside chants, only energy and spirit. That friend's actions spoke louder than words.

The obstacle to healing in the sense of it blocking one from becoming more fully whole or fulfilled can be removed with a relationship and words. If the obstacle to the healing, in the sense of blocking one from becoming more fully whole or fulfilled, can be removed with a relationship and words, this might work both ways. When one helps another heal in this way that benefit redounds back to the healer. This is reciprocal.

And, if it is a two-way process, might this happen from words one exchanges with oneself, with one's relationship with one's Self? (This, too, came to my attention.)

CHAPTER 10

TALKING TO ONESELF:
AN UNDERRATED CONVERSATION

One example

I was in my 60s when I read my Vietnam journal. It was an uncomfortable experience. My discomfort wasn't just my recalling the frustration behind those words written by my former self. It went deeper than that. I'd been educating myself about the Vietnamese people, their history up to and including their years under French rule. My sweeping ignorance and shameful behavior while serving in Vietnam, brought embarrassment with discomfort for much of what that young writer, I once was, wrote. The more mature me felt ashamed.

Revisiting those events I found myself realigning assumptions and labels that appeared in that journal. I wanted to remove inappropriate presumptions and emotions. For example, I found myself reflecting on my new understanding that my Vietnamese counterparts' predecessors, during the early colonial years, had been denied leadership training and experience at the highest levels of administration. How could I not see, appreciate – at least respect – the resentment that surely accompanied that obligatory dependency and denial of critical training and experience? How could I not but respect the inevitable urge for payback? After all, don't I live in Massachusetts, a former colony of a European power, where our "Boston Tea Party," an act of sabotage against the Crown, is remembered and celebrated to this day with righteous patriotic pride?

How did I not see, accept, and appreciate that my Vietnamese colleagues back then might also have been too exhausted and burned-out from their nation's twenty years of uninterrupted fighting, to care? Why had no one pointed out that they may have been simply too depleted after fighting, not for securing democracy for their people but for getting yet another foreign overlord to leave, this time us Americans? And, how could my team and I not have provoked and triggered those issues and that trauma back then, that I was now reading in my journal? I squirm now and feel chagrin and regret. My earlier self-righteous frustration had initially welcomed me when I began reading my journal, but then, my reading between the lines made more and more of it uncomfortable to read, even though it was simultaneously an enlightened and overdue awakening.

For example, when I got to the entry that described how, shortly before my tour of duty was up and while I was still in Banmethuot, I'd been asked by a ranking visitor whether I'd be interested in staying on in the military to help train new doctors being prepared for this MILPHAP mission, I remembered my response. I'd declined, not without a second thought but without even a first thought. Now, reading that journal entry and appreciating that the U.S. military back then was doing the best it could with what it had, and it didn't have that much because of people like me, people more ready to blame than cut slack and recalculate, more eager to leave and return home than stay on and help, I squirmed. I squirmed remembering my brusque dismissal of that request and felt an embarrassment about my sitting on my high horse for so long. I consoled myself with the thought that, at least now, I might be becoming more the person I've known I should be.

CHAPTER 11

OUR BETTER NATURE
AND THE MASCULINE VALENCE

There's a lesson in here, too.

On January 12, 2016, two small U.S. Navy Riverine vessels in the Persian Gulf stray into Iranian territorial waters. They are confronted by the Iranian Coast Guard and the crews are taken into custody. That makes breaking news. The U.S. commander explains to the Iranians that it was a mistake on his part, apologizes and, within 24 hours, the vessels and crew are released. That, too, is breaking news. Under the circumstances of that time and place and the history of US-Iran relations, such a happy outcome is a welcome relief, given the violent alternatives. But what notably lingers in the headlines following the release is the apology. An American military officer apologized?! (The Iranian Press had released a video of that apology which went viral so now the whole world knew.) For the Iranians, the incident was a learning moment, at least that's what Iranian Foreign Minister Javad Zarif, who'd maintained open lines of communication with Secretary of State John Kerry and U.S. officials, wrote in a tweet to Kerry. Making no mention of the apology, Zarif tweeted to the effect that he was happy to see that a dialog and show of respect, instead of threats and impulsiveness, had quickly resolved the sailor episode and that it was a valuable learning moment. But then the event's consequences slipped out of control with news headlines ranging from indignation over the US apology, to denials that there even was an apology, to an interest in whether the Navy Commander who was filmed apologizing would be reprimanded – all variations of a US Navy seriously humiliated.

It was clear to me that it wasn't that an American officer did something rarely done that warranted this attention. It was that what he had done was wrong. But, I'm thinking, isn't admitting you've made a mistake that causes someone concern and worry, and then saying you're sorry, the way we were raised? Isn't that the right thing to do? For us Americans to do? Are we not Number One in respect and good manners, if not common sense, not just strength and power? Must we be Number One in thin skin as well? We know it's the manly thing to do, but must we forever look for excuses or ways to spin a denial or rattle a sword? Apparently and unfortunately, what grabs headlines doesn't just reflect American sensibilities and expectations, it shapes them. It signals that saying you're sorry is simply not the manly thing to do.

Reflecting on this I was reminded how often Our American Story that embodies our high principles places rank and station ahead of relational connections and often places strength through intimidation and control ahead of strength through statesmanship and detente (and good manners). I was reminded how we are all cued towards a masculine bias, having heard my share of stories of the man who remains in a terrible job that is killing him and is respected as a dutiful provider, toughing it out for his family and staying that course, whereas the woman who remains in an abusive marriage is looked upon as foolish and urged to get out. From this perspective, I could see that the Vietnam War, a combination of a killer job joined to a bad marriage, was obviously tilted toward the masculine option wherein we hung in there, hung tough, and did our job despite knowing we'd never win. We delayed leaving Vietnam to sustain our reputation, honor, and world standing as leader. That was what our men and women died for. Looking back, the question doesn't seem to be about whether or not we did save face, reputation, honor, and our standing as world leader. It now appears to be whether those were even in need of saving.

There was a lesson here and I looked for it. I began with the awakening that my own masculine valence was seductive as well as dominant. It reminded me how, in wartime, victory had always been our preferred goal, not detente. Muscle was what mattered, not manners. But the Cold War and the Vietnam War had long been over and subsequent wars had been very different. Friends and foes have not only been difficult to distinguish, they overlap and shift. Our masculine valence hasn't always worked as a go-to posture and those postures of dominance with displays of authority don't seem to bring us anymore to where we need to be. I was re-calculating old verities. An earlier and popular iteration of our exceptionalism was already slipping towards embarrassment-ism.

For my generation, our embarrassment over the Abu Ghraib prison scandal pushed that point in my face. Why, we had asked, should we be so embarrassed for our treatment of a captured enemy? Weren't we treating scum like scum, evil demons as evil demons the way they deserved to be treated? Why should we have to apologize for disrespecting Evil? The reason,

I realized, was that those names, rhetorical devices, and metaphors, ought to be treated as such. They weren't real. They were tools, and we all had forgotten they were tools. Our masculine imperative, it seemed, had simply tuned out the voice of our humanity, our better nature, the voice that knew that acting evil and evil weren't the same.

That lesson was clear to me. Our better nature, our conscience, our moral compass, had automatically snapped back into place after our behavior had been publicly exposed to all Americans, not just a few. As a result, we all stepped back from that masculine imperative. That was the lesson. We all saw our behavior through others' eyes – saw it as a nation – and knew we should be ashamed. We were better than that. That Abu Ghraib prison behavior was unworthy of who we all were, who we wanted to believe we were, and who we knew we ought to be and strive to be, all expressions of our better nature.

This reawakening happened because we Americans must have had what I call "wordless conversations" with ourselves. Everyone's integrity, the bedrock of our better nature, seemed to have been redeemed here. That was certainly true for me, as was the reminder that life throws mean curves in the road ahead and meanings can too easily conceal, as well as enrich, our better natures which can always be better. I was also reminded of what can happen when we begin hitting those mean curves. We can begin demonizing our foes wherein the negativity, of course, rebounds back to us and that's when we begin acting like the demon we saw in the other. What goes around does come around. I know this because I remember how, in my experience, what went around came around.

I was reminded of how I'd felt that first time I read my journal of my Vietnam experience. The good news was that this redounding process was the same for our positive energies as our negative energies. U.S. President Ronald Reagan must have emitted positive energies in his summit meeting with USSR President Gorbachev in May, 1988. That was when the Intermediate-Range Nuclear Force Treaty was signed. It was Reagan the person, Gorbachev said later, and not just the U.S. President and his policies, that softened his position and made that summit a success.

PART V:

BE YOUR MORE COMPLETE SELF
AND SAVE A WORLD –
THE PRESCRIPTION

CHAPTER 12

IMPLEMENTING THE RECIPROCITY
OF HEALING ENCOUNTERS

I had only to look around.

There is reciprocity in healing encounters. Positive energies we emit do rebound back to us.

I mentally gathered my evidence. What was remarkable in my evidence gathering was that it didn't just happen in relationships with people. It happened in relationships with animals. I'll start with that, with my pet dogs throughout my life. My dogs were all happy to see me when I returned home and my seeing tails vigorously wagging made me delighted to be so enthusiastically greeted. It worked the other way as well. When I slapped my leg the dogs always came to me with wagging tails as if in response to the sound of my "wagging tail," created by my leg slapping. To me, looking back, this is simply a two-way reflexion of what I've come to call "positive energies," almost as if it's the way we're wired, my pets and I. I find it easy to imagine an original genetic purpose in early wolves, long before dogs, wherein responses to one another began to insure functioning in packs and reinforcing bonds, all of which supported survival.

As for reciprocity in my relationships with people, that, too, was easy to find. Spontaneous reciprocity. Smiles that reflect a mood of contentment get spread easily in groups or crowds. It is common knowledge that smiles lift spirits and promote our immune systems. The contagion of the annual Christmas holiday spirit is a very good example. As a medical doctor, I've seen how a doctor's smile makes a difference, and how the patient's return smile, whether in acknowledgment, respect, or affirmation, impacts that doctor in return. Something is obviously flowing here in two directions.

Most remarkable but, again, no surprise to me, was this reciprocity occurring in our relationships with inanimate objects. I'm thinking here of the neglected child cuddling a doll and who, for that moment of cuddling, doesn't feel neglected because, at those moments, it's as if she is that doll. I'm thinking, too, of the small boy going to daycare carrying his Batman action figure and feeling secure, as if it is his hero holding his hand. And I'm remembering, too, how the practice of psychoanalysis, which is anchored in the effort to draw out and bottle, so to speak, and then share and study the phenomenon of "as if" connections, advances understanding and insights into a person's experience and behaviors. The goal of that treatment, of course, is to help a person become more self-aware, more whole.

My favorite example is my relationship with our living and sensitive ecosystem. The more we demonstrate respect for our ecosystem the more it redounds to our credit in terms of the food we eat, the water we drink, and the clothes we wear, not to mention the weather that sustains all of these.

Finally, I must add, I see it happening in my relationship with myself (and I don't think I'm alone here). Aren't we always in conversation with ourselves? I think of myself walking along the street and passing a store window and glancing at my reflection, or sitting quietly and struggling with a crisis to get a handle on my thoughts and feelings in order to respond. I think, too, of looking into a mirror at home, or daydreaming while shooting hoops. I've come to consider all these as conversations, see them as dialogues with myself even if I'm not forming words or am just experiencing a mood. Doesn't everybody come to decisions and find resolve and hope this way? As I've come to see it, while these conversations with ourselves may appear to be one-way, they are not. We're listening too. We "hear."

Putting these observations and personal experiences together, how can I not help thinking about poets and our relationship with mirrors? And, who hasn't been uplifted listening to the lyrics of the song written by George Weiss and Bob Thiele and made famous by Louis Armstrong, that embodies just such an internal dialogue: "I see trees of green, red roses too. I see them bloom for me and you. And I think to myself, what a wonderful world." And I can't help reminding myself that the Jewish prayer, "The Shema," arguably the most important part of our prayer service, is not directed at God but to the people, themselves. This, too, is a manifestation of exercising this reciprocity of word-borne energies and powers that flow two ways.

One point, I had to keep reminding myself, was that the opposite is also true. It too, is also easily forgotten. Disrespecting, if not demonizing, the other easily becomes the norm, and is easily anchored in our toxic comfort zone. Whether we do this in our personal lives, social lives, athletic, or political lives, we become unafraid this way. We are unafraid to disrespect the other and that's big. Putting down the other seems to have become our formal expression of justice and righteousness, of strength and honor. But, I'm also suspecting, if our goal is to be the healing of our nation, and healing is a variation of becoming more complete or whole, then we, ourselves, must heal, too. We must become more whole ourselves. But, if venting and feeling good, especially by getting the other to feel bad, is our preferred modus operandi, healing just isn't going to happen. Worse. Our show of disrespect for the other is what will redound to us; we'll have just disrespected our own humanity and, from there, it's a slippery slope.

For me, memories of moments on that slippery slope still come easily to mind, especially when featuring our leaders. Even distant memories. I'm remembering President H.W. Bush and our cheering response when, on the deck of the aircraft carrier USS Abraham Lincoln in 2003, he led our celebration. We had a military success and we happily passed the misery on to the other side. That misery, of course, redounded back to us in spades. Do we not have more enemies now than we had then? Negative energy, our disrespecting of another, does that. "Screw you" invariably invites, "Screw me? Screw *you!*" – a posture that at times proves fatal.

CHAPTER 13

REDEEMING THE OTHER'S SELF-RESPECT REDOUNDS BACK TO US

Simple and doable while also formidable.

Midrash on Genesis 38, The Power of Words

There is a specific moment in the biblical account of Judah and Tamar wherein each is at their most vulnerable, and where, for each, things couldn't be worse. Then, they *do* become worse. Judah's integrity and honor have long hovered near his bottom. Now he is about to commit yet another dishonorable act, this one egregious. Tamar, who has lost not only two husbands but also her rightful compensation and family connection with a marriage to Judah's third son, Shelah, is now about to lose her life. She's to be executed.

We recall how this crisis came about. Tamar had disguised herself as a prostitute and engineered an encounter with Judah. She had an agenda. Judah, not recognizing her, had sex with her compounding his record of dishonorable deeds. It seems that not seeing behind masks, was, for him, a well-exercised habit. He didn't see who his sex partner really was; he didn't even see who he really was.

Now the fix is on, to use a sports gambling expression that is remarkably apt here because, in one sense of that word, they're both "in a fix" (a mess), and in the other sense (healing), they are both in need of serious "fixing."

We recall how it plays out. In her prostitute guise Tamar demands and receives as payment for sex, Judah's seal, cord, and staff. Then, when she, Tamar, a widow, is visibly and publicly pregnant, Judah, her father-in-law finds out and, unaware he was the one who impregnated her, orders that she be put to death, that being the honorable thing to do. Now, Tamar acts. Presenting Judah's seal, cord, and staff to her would-be executioner, she declares, "I am with child by the man to whom these belong. Examine these:

whose seal and cord and staff are these?"[6] Judah, hearing these words, passes his tipping point and moves towards transformation with self-recognition. We can almost envision that scene in slow-motion, where Tamar's words jumpstart in Judah's mind that long blocked-out memory of his presenting his own father, Jacob, with his brother's bloodied coat with similar words, "We found this. Please examine it; is it your son's tunic or not?"[7] This was followed by his cruel lie that the blood on Joseph's coat was Joseph's, not that of a goat, and then followed by his denial of any opportunity of feeling remorse by closing off such memories from his conscious awareness. Split-screen: this is the same instant when Judah realizes that his daughter-in-law, Tamar, is that prostitute that he, himself, impregnated, her words being the tipping-point for her recognition and redemption. Judah's self-recognition is, thus, joined to his recognition of Tamar as a whole person, a desperate daughter-in-law twice widowed and to whom so much was owed and continued to be owed, and who has here desperately, audaciously, and triumphantly faced down her adversary. "She is more in the right than I," Judah realizes, "inasmuch as I did not give her to my son, Shelah."[8] It's as if the words Tamar had spoken to the executioner to be delivered to Judah bore powerful energies, energies that ultimately redounded to her credit, as well as penetrated their primary target, Judah. These were energies that healed.

My 21st Century Midrash Takeaway

Illuminating a blind spot and seeing at last what had been looked at before without being seen, can be transformative. This, I found, was especially true if the blind spot had served to hide from one's awareness something unsavory such as one's misdeeds. Its illumination can be so much more memorable as well as truthful with enhanced self-awareness. This, then, is one way that transformation and reform can be achieved.

More to my point, I saw how an enhanced respect for oneself (here, Judah) can mirror a respect for another (here, Tamar), and vice-versa. One's respect for the other (here, Judah's for Tamar) also mirrors one's respect for one's self (here, Judah's emerging self-respect). I interpreted this as a reciprocity wherein

---

6. JPS Tanakh: The Holy Scriptures: The New JPS Translation According to the Traditional Hebrew Text (Pennsylvania: The Jewish Publication Society, 1985), (1) Genesis 38–25 p. 1.

7. Ibid. (Genesis 37:32) p.60.

8. Ibid. (Genesis 38:26) p. 61.

healing energies flow in two directions. (We already know that destructive energies flow two ways; e.g. our instinctive, knee-jerk impulses to "get back" and "get even.")

In terms of my quest, my conscious effort to maximize my own measure of wholeness, this meant at the very least neutralizing the word-toxins and disrespectful labels and smears that I apply in my thoughts as well as speech. Of course, I could and would still use those terms, but now they'd be prefaced with, "as if." (e.g. He is, "as if," the Devil.) In addition, I'd only apply them to the other's behavior, never their humanity. To my satisfaction I found this not only easy to remember, I found it unexpectedly satisfying. The other fellow's sense of Self would be safe in encounters with me.

In short, I was ensuring that I'd always distinguish metaphor from reality. My need to vent would remain intact, of course. Loving my enemies would continue to be unnecessary and forgiving them, would be a non-existing goal. In contrast, calling them Evil, even in my head, was the lurking slippery slope. In my contacts with others as well as in my thoughts, my better nature should always be addressing the other's better nature.

Taking it to the next level, humanity was the cornerstone of what I've come to call our "better nature." (It was also obvious that, for some people, a "better nature" could not be acknowledged, let alone applied, and for a reason. For some, it may have been there but at times was severely wounded and crushed; even buried.) My show of respect to that other person's better nature – wounded, crushed, or buried though it may be – would still be my path to further enriching my sense of Self by enriching the other's. If I could save his or her "world," even for a moment, I'd still be saving mine – ours – at least for that moment, and, after all, isn't that precisely what's necessary if we are to get ourselves back on our feet?

CHAPTER 14

THE SHOW OF RESPECT
IS WHAT STARTS THAT BALL ROLLING

Yes. Acting and pretending are acceptable.

Midrash on Genesis 38, Manipulating and Doctoring

In summary, for the transfer of healing energies to happen, Tamar had to pretend to be a fallen woman, someone who'd hit bottom. It was an act and insincere, of course, but by virtue of this act she was able to manipulate Judah in a way that, not only did he hit bottom, he *knew* he hit bottom. There'd be no blocking this out of his awareness. His mask wouldn't prop him "up-right" this time.

My 21st Century Midrash Takeaway

Sometimes one has to hit bottom before there can be a turning and rising up, which leads to this remarkable take-home lesson. Pretending – speaking and acting "as if" – can and does function as an effective catalyst in the service of healing, and the healing of one person might just be what saves the world of another.

Here is the good news and there's a kicker as well.

My prescription, I'd discovered, may take the form of acting. Yes, acting. We can pretend. We can pretend that we mean what we say. We can act as if we understand, care, and forgive. We play that role. We can act out those conversations, those shows we put on. And, yes, even for ourselves because we, too, are being listened to here. We are being listened to through other parts of ourselves – if not the judgmental parts, then the neglected parts, the frightened parts, the silenced and the hopeful parts. We are heard.

It turns out that this show of respect, this pretense, does redound to our merit and self-respect. It does redound to our integrity.

Where does this notion come from? Where do we get off believing that letting go of toxic words of disrespect and addressing others with a show of respect invites any self-respect? Where is it written that pretending, even to ourselves, a respectfulness we don't actually feel – that acting as if we understand, care, and forgive even others driven entirely by beliefs and feelings instead of thoughtful and studied facts – actually earns us respect for ourselves? Who am I to say that insincere, albeit respectful, behavior towards another redounds to our merit with a dividend of self-respect and, from this, a restored integrity that tempers our defensiveness? Where does such a convoluted trail of connected dots come from?

For me, *they come from everyday experience*. And I don't think it's just me. Who hasn't personally appreciated the power words carry, including words spoken to ourselves (and represented so sweetly and memorably by the mantra, "I think I can. I think I can" from the children's book, *The Little Engine That Could,* by Watty Piper)? Who hasn't personally appreciated how "positive self-talk," as some call it, improves one's performance as well as one's health? There is even an experiment whereby a random group is instructed to start laughing. They start laughing fake laughter and, in time, that fake laughter becomes genuine laughter. It's true. Acting as if one is having fun does actually become fun. When you factor in that humor and laughter are "good medicine" – thinking of the boost our laughter gives to our immune systems and the regular clown visits scheduled nowadays at children's hospital wards – the phenomenon becomes familiar. There are even studies of actors whose performances involve acting as if they were severely depressed such as in a stage play and then, following those performances, their blood test results show chemical changes associated with actual depression. Think of the insecure job applicant with low confidence. There are studies that demonstrate that, such a person, after assuming the pose and gestures that naturally follow victory in the boxing ring or on the playing field but here, assuming them *prior* to a job interview… that pre-interview experience generates *actual* self-confidence that one then experiences during that interview.

They come from moments when we witness a small gesture of respect and caring offered by one stranger to another at the park or beach, or at an accident site along the highway, or watching a video on the evening news of such behavior at the site of a terrorist bombing or earthquake when we find ourselves moved, sometimes to tears. Are we all not, at such moments and on some level, putting ourselves into the shoes of one of those strangers? Is that not a form of vicarious acting "as if"? *In fact, isn't all empathy a form of vicarious acting "as if"?* Tears of empathy relate to healing, not sorrow.

Psychiatry training taught me that behavior change follows insight but my practice taught me that the reverse can be more true. Insight, I found, can follow behavior change. In other words, sometimes we must first do the right thing before we are able to understand and appreciate why. The Bible text, after all, reads, "Observe and hear all these words which I command thee" (Deut. 12:28)? It is translated as, "Observe and hear," not "Hear and observe."

I've heard talk about the loss of innocence that comes with the impact of war, as if such innocence is gone, never to return. But, what if some part of that innocence remains, called by another name perhaps, or masquerading as something else, buried somewhere inside us? What if it reappears from time to time for brief moments? Like when a puppy on your lap looks up and you instinctively touch it. Or, when you see the Disney movie, *Pinocchio* and, when the puppet learns he's earned the right to be a real boy, your eyes water. What if our loss of integrity and the silence of our better natures are like that? What if they can be lost or broken for a moment, even appear to be lost or broken for the rest of our lives, but for moments one can almost see their shadow or catch their spirit because they're not totally lost or permanently broken? They're only battered or temporarily depleted, or just, for the time being, compromised and silenced. What if it's true that when we are listening to our better nature and our better nature is touching others, we have temporarily stepped out of the way of our own healing and, for a moment, have a feeling of hope and confidence in what lies ahead – in the world ahead? Have we not, for a moment anyway, "saved a world"? To me, what all this means is that our removing the toxicity from our civil discourse will be a gradual process. It will be, perhaps, person to person and moment to moment.

And there's this tag-along memory: I was almost a teen. A group of older kids – "the big kids" we used to call them, or "the bullies" when they chased us home from school, wanting to take something from us or push us down and scare us – cornered me with their bikes in a neighborhood far from home. I hadn't a chance. I was scared. It was by instinct that I deliberately showed no fear and, before any of them spoke, asked about their bikes. Cornered by their bikes and unable to move, but now focusing on their bikes, what followed was conversation, sharing, and friendliness. Then they left. It is only now that I am able to reframe that experience as one in which the other's better nature responded to my own. My show of interest and respect were all bogus. It was that memory of my showing respect (not feeling it) that nailed down this "prescription." A show of respect spared me humiliation, a broken bike, and an urge to get even.

Again, what I'm talking about isn't something learned. It was instinctive. Again, none of this need be new. There are already more than a few aphorisms and proverbs that put what I'm saying in context and that honor its purpose, ranging from, "One good turn deserves another" to "What goes around comes around." Jewish tradition has phrased it, "Our wishing someone well earns God's blessing." And there are the wordless renditions as well, the facial expressions, gestures, and body positions that come to us so naturally... as if that, too, is in our wiring and that, too, is linked to a pre-sapien survival instinct.

CHAPTER 15

POSTSCRIPT: A FISSURE-VARIANT

Where unspoken words and imaginary relationships
provide moments of healing and peace.

There were other corruptions of ethics with integrity loss in the Vietnam War era. Unlike by me, those other violators sometimes had no partners for bonding and blaming once back in the States and, to their disadvantage, no blind spot either, meaning they carried their burden of guilt alone and never forgotten. Their conversations were often without words, just feelings and reactions. Their relationships were sometimes fleeting. For many, that burden was deadly as well as intolerable. But, for some, they became restorative, if only temporarily.

I include this in my memoir because it confirms my prescription. It's the same prescription, the show of respect redounds and, at least for a moment, quiets a toxic storm.

The following are from information gathered, memoir notes, and conversations with myself.

The Vietnam Veterans Memorial, dedicated on Veterans Day, 1982, was conceived by veterans and constructed without government funds thus generating controversy from the start. How could a daughter of Chinese immigrants, still only a student, be the winner of a nationwide design competition? How could a black granite slab in the ground with names of American war dead inscribed on it be a fitting way to honor those who made the ultimate sacrifice? How could something so heart-wrenching serve as a military memorial with nothing heroic or uplifting about it? How could such a flawed memorial, where you look into blackness and see only names and your own reflection, represent who we were and what we did, or who we are and aspire to be?

But, visitors keep coming. They stand and look. They touch the wall and cry, it is *that* powerful, *that* moving. It is there to experience, not just see. A replica even travels the country, it has become that popular. What explains this connection with American people? Could it be that, for a moment, for some, touching the wall, a name, bridges a divide, a divide between past and present, the living and dead? Is that what this memorial, part in the ground, part above the ground, means? That divides can be bridged? That we can reach across and touch and be touched? That healing energies actually flow in both directions? That seeing one's own reflection and looking at it is a conversation?

Maybe it took someone outside the box of our narrative shield to see what was called for, someone young and new to our American Story, someone who could see that this was the season for healing, for redemption, and that reconciliation and finding peace can begin from the ground up and through a personal experience; a conversation, actually. And maybe it required a panel of judges who appreciated how pain not only accompanies injury, it accompanies the healing as well.

What are those veterans saying to those names and reflected images in their conversations at that wall? Or, are they simply looking both at the names and at their own reflections, respectfully, and listening with their hearts? What are they feeling? These are conversations about grieving, about solemnly and, for many, respectfully making an offering, a sacrifice, letting something go, like a teddy bear, wedding ring, military badge, a medal; flowers, flags, dog tags; books, artwork, a walking stick; clothing and handwritten notes, along with sorrow and tears. (Items left at the wall since its dedication in November 1982, numbering more than 400,000.) Sometimes it is only by letting something go that we find room for letting something in.

I see healing happening here, if only for moments. What probably matters for many is simply knowing that they belong here at that wall that mirrors them, and that speaks to them as well as for them. For some, there may be nowhere else where they feel expected and so totally accepted, so totally in the right company. Many have left where they live to come to this place to respectfully share, in silent conversation, as it were, even for a brief moment, their isolation, helplessness, misery, grief, and, yes, guilt and remorse, vulnerability and fear. For a moment they have taken themselves enough out of the way of healing to experience a respectful moment. For that moment, as I see it now, there has been a two-way conversation anchored in a respectful connection.

I can't help thinking now about those veterans suffering from what are arguably among the most treatment-resistant of mental wounds, veterans who are least likely to heal and move on. These are the veterans whose anger, guilt, and blame are directed, not at their leaders, or the media, or anti-war activists, or even at the enemy, but at themselves. These are the military men who deliberately committed or abetted heinous atrocities on helpless, innocent unarmed civilians. Unlike the rest of us, they are not stuck in this valley, they are stuck in hell. Professionals in Veterans Administration facilities have tried to help these veterans in different ways. In one way the veterans are encouraged to look inward and accept their guilt and remorse. This is their suggested path to healing and moving on. It doesn't help. Another way of helping those Vietnam veterans is to focus on the wider context and try to accept and take solace in the knowledge that they aren't entirely at fault. Our violent culture at home as well as abroad – recalling the Watts Riots and Civil Rights Marches back then – and the lowering of standards for acceptance into the draft, for example, can make the wider system at least somewhat complicit in their behavior and mental states. That, too, doesn't help. But, I've read that there are moments of healing and respite that come, not in the presence of therapists but in the presence of fellow veterans, warriors similarly tainted who accept one another into their company and share their anguish and grief. Embraced by this unique, special, and temporary community where they are figuratively, if not literally, embraced, it's as if, at the times these groups meet, and for brief moments, they can relax their desperate grip on their isolation and solitude, their shield that has, for so long and so effectively spared them from something even worse, the terror of madness, of disintegration of Self, the ultimate loss of integrity where only suicide brings relief. It is as if, for the moments those veterans are together to respectfully acknowledge one another as they are and have been, to reveal their more complete selves, the world becomes, for that moment anyway, their world, too.

APPENDIX I

CHAPTER 4: INTEGRITY IS EVERYWHERE UNDER FIRE

And seeds of bonding and blaming began taking root.

Among Early Advisors

For the early period of U.S. Military Advisors in Vietnam 1955–1965 (the Military Assistance Command Vietnam, MACV, wasn't formed until 1962), there was a bind between cultivating a relationship with a Vietnamese counterpart which obliged turning a blind eye to his or her corrupt practices versus making the welfare of the Vietnamese people the priority which, of course, risked spoiling that collegial relationship. One couldn't dodge this; one had to choose. Ought you cultivate political bonds that shows America trusts a weak, ineffective, failing and increasingly unpopular Saigon leadership at the expense of the Vietnamese people as well as the security of our own men considering that Vietcong had infiltrated that leadership to the highest levels? Or, ought it be the interests of the Vietnamese people that comes first? Ought you intervene or at least report when you see American aid diverted to line pockets of corrupt officials, or ought you turn a blind eye inasmuch as our State Department and President already know about this and want the American people kept in the dark? Inaction gives the appearance we are putting the Saigon government first, so inaction itself threatens our relationship with the peasants in the countryside for whom so much of that stuff, now on the black market, is intended. What's the priority? Is it our relationship with the unpopular but anti-communist government in Saigon? Or is it our relationship with the apolitical peasants in the countryside who provide the Vietcong sanctuary for any number of reasons?

The poignancy of this choice was captured by Tim O'Brien's assessment of himself when he confronted his own ethical bind. Here he is, a twenty-two-year-old college graduate receiving his draft notice and facing two options.

Either he submits to the draft, goes, fights, and possibly kills or is killed in a war he believes to be wrong, or follow his conscience, and flee to Canada. "I was a coward," he explains. "I went to war."[9]

At MACV Headquarters

Given MACVs dual objective of finding and killing the enemy along with winning the hearts and minds of the people to their government, consider the following rundown of U.S. military rules of engagement.

"First, if American troops were fired upon from a South Vietnamese village, they could call in a bombing strike on the village immediately and without warning. Even a single round of sniper fire from the general vicinity of a village could lead to the destruction of the entire village.

"Second, if the United States had evidence that villagers were providing support to the Vietcong or North Vietnamese Army (food, housing, information, etc.) the entire village could be destroyed. The rules required that the village be given a warning in advance 'whenever possible.' The warning might come from helicopter loudspeakers or leaflets dropped from the sky. But since the 'warnings' were often couched as a general ultimatum, villagers had no idea if or when they would be bombed.

"Third, areas from which civilians had been forcibly removed were declared free-fire zones. The U.S. rules of engagement authorized the random destruction of anything that remained or returned. Most of those villages were then burned, bombed, or bulldozed. Yet many Vietnamese found their displacement so intolerable they returned to their destroyed villages despite the risk of living in areas the United States claimed a right to obliterate repeatedly."[10]

These rules, leaning heavily on the attrition objective, not only downplay the political objective of winning support from the apolitical peasants in the countryside for their Saigon government, they ignore it. These rules provide no protections whatsoever for the property and lives of civilians. Worse, they place villagers in someone's crosshairs and they can't escape. They have no choice. How are unarmed farmers supposed to persuade armed and committed Vietcong intruders to leave their villages? Effectively, their hearts and minds,

---

9. Tim O'Brien, *The Things They Carried* (London: Penguin Books, 1990), p. 63.

10. Christian G. Appy, *American Reckoning: The Vietnam War and Our National Identity* (London: Penguin Books, 2015), p. 167.

if not their entire village, are what take the hit as these rules about how to implement these dual objectives, trickle down to the on-the-ground decision-makers. One officer's alleged spin on the justification for the destruction of the entire village of Ben Tre reveals how the corruption of one's integrity can actually masquerade as a virtue. "That village had to be destroyed," this unidentified major is alleged to have reported to AP correspondent Peter Arnett in one terse, unattributed article, "in order to save it."[11]

Similar rules of engagement, for all branches of service, not only gave moral legitimacy to such brutalization of South Vietnamese civilians, folks who were our allies and who would determine the legitimacy for any Saigon government, those rules converted American participants into thugs, arguably complicit in war crimes.

On the Ground

The following account during the post-TET U.S. counteroffensive, points in this same direction. American Lt. Tobias Wolff, an adviser to an ARVN artillery battalion near the town of My Tho, recalls:

"We knocked down bridges and sank boats. We leveled shops and bars along the river. We pulverized hotels and houses, floor by floor, street by street, block by block. I saw the map. I knew where the shells were going but I didn't think of our targets as homes where exhausted and frightened people were praying for their lives."[12]

The air force subsequently joins in to bomb whatever targets the artillery missed. The lieutenant's narrative continues:

"Only when we finally took the town back… did I see what we had done, we and the VC together. The place was a wreck, still smoldering two weeks later, still reeking sweetly of corpses. The corpses were everywhere, lying in the streets, floating in the reservoir… the smell so thick and foul we had to wear surgical masks scented with cologne, aftershave, deodorant, whatever we had, simply to move through the town…. Hundreds of corpses and the count kept rising…. One day I passed a line of them that went on for almost a block, all children."[13]

It was common knowledge that the VC would deliberately come into

---

11. http://aphelis.net/destroy-village-order-save-unknown-1968/.
12. Tobias Wolff, *In Pharaoh's Army* (New York: Vintage Books, 1994), p. 138.
13. Ibid. p. 138.

towns like My Tho knowing this is precisely what would happen. The lieutenant explains:

"In this way they taught the people that we did not love them and would not protect them; that for all our talk of partnership and brotherhood we disliked and mistrusted them and that we would kill every last one of them to save our own skins."[14]

Taint, the mark of corruption, proves contagious. From the contradictory set of expectations to the biased rules of engagement to the troops who had to implement them, the taint spreads up to the general whose request for more troops is finally denied. What happens next is what happens whenever something contagious, like a virus, isn't contained and eliminated. General Westmoreland turns and reveals his own contamination by blaming America's civilian leadership along with the press for the failure to "win." Ultimately, truth itself becomes tainted, the truth being that no amount of violence and carnage on the U.S. part is capable of winning legitimacy for any Saigon government, the sine-qua-non for victory.

Corruption by the mid-1960s had become a culture that spread orally, by word of mouth. It is 1967. You are the information officer at the headquarters of the 25th Division at Cu Chi orienting a newly arrived, inexperienced war correspondent. You are explaining details on a map on your wall that features the Ho Bo Woods, the site of recent military action. Do you provide a full picture to that correspondent that includes the way that destructive action at the Ho Bo Woods impacted the long-term success of the U.S. mission by fouling any future support of undecided peasants in that area for their government, support that's a must for a U.S. victory? Or do you limit your explanation to the immediate, short-term impact and the boost that provides a concerned domestic readership? The officer at Ho Bo goes with the latter and does so with such gusto – he takes the journalist up in a helicopter to view the damage close up – that gusto was, arguably, what earned him this role of interpreter of U.S. action in Vietnam to the world. Here's what that journalist, a young Michael Herr, wrote about that encounter.

"I met an information officer... who showed me on his map... what they'd done to the Ho Bo Woods, the vanished Ho Bo Woods, taken off by giant Roma plows and chemicals and long, slow fire, wasting hundreds of acres

---

14. Ibid.

of cultivated plantation and wild forest alike, 'denying the enemy valuable resources and cover.'"[15]

Herr continues:

"It had been part of his (information officer) job for nearly a year now to tell people about that operation – the correspondents, touring congressmen, movie stars, corporation presidents, staff officers from half the armies in the world, and he still couldn't get over it. It seemed to be keeping him young. His enthusiasm made you feel that even the letters he wrote home to his wife were full of it, it really showed what you could do if you had the know-how and the hardware. And if in the months following that operation, indices of enemy activity in the larger areas of War Zone C had increased 'significantly,' and American losses had doubled and then doubled again, none of it was happening in any damn Ho Bo Woods, you'd better believe it...."[16]

That taint rebounds back on itself and reinforces the core corruption as in this incident. A seasoned combat trooper seeks to re-enlist saying he can't hack it back home in the States. This would be a red flag if it were an initial enlistment, not a re-enlistment he was seeking, even if he'd never mentioned that he'd sit all day in his room at home, sometimes sticking a hunting rifle out the window and aiming at people and cars, frightening his parents. Either way, whoever stands to accept and forward his re-enlistment papers has a choice between this impaired soldier's need for healing and the army's need for battle-tested troops wherein, whatever you chose, an important value will be struck down. Outcome? That soldier is accepted for a third tour in Vietnam. What happens next, according to journalist Herr is this.

"... he put people uptight here too, even here."[17]

"'No man, I'm sorry, he's just too crazy for me,' one of the men in his team said. 'All's you got to do is look in his eyes, that's the whole f***ing story right there."[18]

"'Yeah, but you better do it (look at him) quick,' someone else said. 'I mean, you don't want to let him catch you at it.'"[19]

One frequently repeated joke bearing on this assault on our integrity takes what is intolerable and pushes it to its ridiculous extreme so we can at least look at it and laugh, because by laughing we create distance and feel a

---

15. Michael Herr, *Dispatches* (New York: Alfred A. Knopf, 197), p. 4.
16. Ibid. p. 4.
17. Ibid. p. 5.
18. Ibid. p. 6.
19. Ibid.

perverse mastery over it. It doesn't scare us to death, that frightful reality that, while this is a war we can't win, as long as we keep up the killing and destruction they can't either, so we keep killing and destroying and dying, and that's the plan. And this is the joke.

"What you do (to achieve victory) is you load all the Friendlies onto ships and take them out to the South China Sea. Then you bomb the country flat. Then you sink the ships."[20]

This is what Integrity-Missing-In-Action is beginning to look like. There is a military sweep out of Song Be with gunships providing air cover, arguably inspired not by evidence of enemy activity but by a commander's desire to impress a visiting war correspondent.

"'Come on,' the captain said, 'we'll take you (journalist) out to play Cowboys and Indians.' We walked out from Song Be in a long line, maybe a hundred men; rifles, heavy automatics, mortars, portable one-shot rocket-launchers, radios, medics, breaking into some kind of sweep formation, five files with small teams of specialists in each file. A gunship flew close hover-cover until we came to some low hills, then two more ships came along and peppered the hills until we'd passed safely through them."[21]

There were no incidents. But then,

"...someone on the point got something – a 'scout,' they thought, and then they didn't know... The captain thought about it during the walk back, but when we got to camp he put it in his report, "One VC killed; good for the unit, he said, not bad for the captain either."[22]

The war culture, it would seem, was now refining, if not informing, the operational rules of engagement. It was no longer the other way around. Again, from Herr:

"In I and II Corps it was 'loose policy' for gunships to fire if the subjects froze down there (while) in the Delta it was to shoot if they ran or 'evaded,' either way a heavy dilemma. Which would you do? 'Air sports,' one gunship pilot called it, and went on to describe it with fervor, 'Nothing finer, you're up there at two thousand, you're God, just open up the flexies and watch it pee, nail those slime to the paddy wall, nothing finer, double back and get the caribou.'"[23]

---

20. Ibid. p. 59.
21. Ibid. p. 61.
22. Ibid.
23. Ibid. p. 62.

In the Air

Identifying targets from the air can be difficult, especially when flying at fast speeds. A decision has to be made, often with limited data. The following exchange between a pilot and ground control, as recalled by Jonathan Schell, a reporter who was there in the plane, illustrates this conundrum and bind, and the ad hoc compromise that ensued. The commander on the ground is guiding Captain Reese to the target by describing it in relation to landmarks visible from the air.

"… 'It's five hundred meters east of that pagoda on the road there. Have you got the pagoda?' the ground commander asked. Captain Reese… answered, 'I see a church but no pagoda.' 'It's right under you now.' 'I don't see it.' 'O.K. Well, there's one hootch down there about a klick south of us that we want you to get. We've got sniper fire out of that tree line.' Captain Reese flew over the area indicated and found that it was occupied by a village of sixty or seventy houses…. 'I see a village down there,' he said. 'No, this is just one hootch,' said the ground commander who was apparently unable to see the village from his spot on the ground because of a thick cover of trees…. (After more discussion and the firing of some marker rockets without success:) 'That's the general area,' said the ground commander apparently tired of trying to pinpoint the one house. 'Do you want us to pretty well cover this general area?' Captain Reese asked. 'Affirmative. Hit the whole area. We've seen activity all through this area.' 'O.K. I'll put a can of napalm and see what it looks like.'… 'Any civilians in the area are Charlies or Charlie sympathizers, so there's no sweat there.'"[24]

Inside the Air Force

Colonel Jack Broughton is in a bind. Two of his four pilots return from a bombing mission to destroy enemy antiaircraft sites and they report accidentally strafing a Soviet ship in Cam Pha port. Such an act is forbidden. The rules of engagement are deliberately restrictive to avoid precisely such a potential provocation. China and the Soviet Union must not be drawn into this conflict. Should the colonel report it or say nothing? The forms pilots fill out after each air strike, every sortie, have no space for reporting

---

24. Jonathan Schell, *The Military Half: An Account of Destruction in Quant Ngai and Quentin* (New York: Alfred A. Knopf, 1968), pp. 172–173.

civilian damage. Besides, the only evidence is the gun-camera film showing the ship in its sights. What's Broughton's priority to be, the solidarity and morale of his team, their confidence in him as wing commander, especially in the face of combat duties that place them at a serious disadvantage, what he'd considered "probably the most inefficient and self-destructive set of rules of engagement that a fighting force ever tried to take into battle"?[25] He has only to destroy the film. Or, as commander, ought he report and punish the offending pilot? He destroys the film.

Inside a Court Martial

For the officers sitting in judgment at Colonel Broughton's subsequent court-martial, it is the same bind. (The Soviets complained of the assault. The President dismissed their complaints but, during the investigation, Broughton confessed.) The court now has to decide which has the higher value – the rules of engagement and the conduct of an officer, or the morale of the fighting men? More, if Broughton and his pilots are to be punished should it be mild, like a reprimand, or severe? The court, seriously divided, finds a way to finesse this conundrum and honor both principles because, at a court-martial – as opposed to in the thick of things – there is time for discussion and debate and consideration of consequences, as well as policy, precedent, and procedure. (They acquit the airmen of conspiring to violate the rule forbidding the bombing of Cam Pha harbor. Broughton is found guilty of destroying government property, the seven rolls of film, and fined $600. He is admonished and transferred to an administrative post in Washington. A year later, his court-martial is expunged from his records.)

Buried in the Numbers Crunched at Rear Echelon Desks

Think of the junior officers in Saigon receiving negative reports from the field but being directed by superiors to tweak these into positive reports before sending them on. Washington has made clear it expects positive reports. It needs them. It's what the president needs the American people to hear. It's a political thing and your career is on the line. In fact, if a commander reports low body counts it is understood that there is a penalty, a poor fitness report, or being passed over for promotion. Besides, who is there to turn to, Washington? So officers lie, while men in the field like combat medic Wayne Smith, are incredulous at the whole attrition concept. "I could not believe my country was capable of going in and killing people," Smith recalls, "and counting their bodies and claiming a victory because we killed more of them than they did of us. There was a real incentivizing of death," he concludes, "and it just f***ed with our value system."[26]

Doctoring the figures becomes standard operating procedure and the figures show we're winning. At any rate, these figures do not show us losing. Not at all.

When evidence accrues that the bombing of the North isn't accomplishing the strategic objective, the measure of success of our airstrikes is simply re-set in terms of numbers of sorties flown and tonnage of ordinance delivered, not targets hit or objectives achieved. It is in this spirit that the measure of success for our civic action programs in winning the people's loyalty to their government, shifts now to body counts of enemy dead.

If the U.S. had considered and applied communist Vietnamese sensibilities as a guide to Hanoi's tipping point instead of American sensibilities, perhaps we'd have foreseen that our bombing would only strengthen the enemy's resolve and lift their morale, not the opposite. Perhaps we wouldn't have continued flogging this drowning horse for as long as we did.

Of course, with presidents, ethical binds go with the job. There is a cabinet and there are advisers and there is time allotted to help with priority-setting and decision-making. There's also a press secretary to help with the spin for public consumption. But, for the low-level officer and the grunts on the ground, there are none of these. There has been no training and there will be no guidance or support. Naturally, something has to give and something does give. Integrity.

Inside Province Hospitals

Not all compromises involving life or death decisions included combat. Think of those American doctors who, like me, were assigned to the Vietnamese health system as part of a State Department counter-insurgency program, MILPHAP (Military Provincial Hospital Assistance Program),[27]

---

26. Christian G. Appy, op. cit. pp. 169–170.
27. Lawrence H. Climo, *The Patient Was Vietcong: An American Doctor in the Vietnamese Health Service* (N. Carolina: McFarland & Company, 1966–1967).

aiming to win the hearts and minds of people to their Saigon government. As described earlier, the doctors' orders were to support the customary medical practice of their Vietnamese counterparts while their Hippocratic Oath as physicians directed them, above all else, to "do no harm," but the reality was that customary Vietnamese practice was causing harm. To intervene and save lives would make the Vietnamese medical staff look bad and the Vietnamese counterparts knew this and didn't want to look bad so they resisted advice to make changes. Those American doctors then had to choose. What was to be their priority, making their counterparts look good or helping their patients get well? What was to be their priority, their orders as officers or their oath as physicians? Obeying either violated the other with consequences to either their political-military mission or their professional integrity and self-worth.

At the Pentagon

General Westmoreland, Commander of all American forces in Vietnam, is under pressure from General Earle Wheeler, Chairman of the Joint Chiefs of Staff, to conceal information that shows that the enemy forces have been increasing in number, giving the lie to claims of U.S. attrition "success." It seems Westmoreland had, all along, been claiming progress by doctoring estimated enemy strength to low numbers which would make the percent of enemy killed high and thus promote that perception of military progress through attrition. Wheeler has cabled Westmoreland to alert him. "If these (true) figures (of enemy troop strength) should reach the public domain they would, literally, blow the lid off Washington," he writes. "Please do whatever is necessary to ensure these figures are not – repeat not – released to the news media."[28] What is Westmoreland to do? The year before, 1966, the CIA estimated the enemy number to be at 600,000 whereas Westmoreland's MACV had reported that enemy number to be 280,000. Now, it's a year later, late 1967; what should Westmoreland report? Should he accept the CIA report, bite that bullet, and admit that the percent of enemy killed is actually very low? Or stick to his guns, "stay the course" he'd set for himself and for MACV and the war where that percentage of enemy killed comes out higher? He stays the course, and stands by his "doctoring" that puts enemy forces below now 240,000. (The TET Offensive begins several months later. He resigns shortly afterward.)

---

28. Christian G. Appy, op. cit. p. 170.

Among Joint Chiefs of Staff

Khe Sanh is under attack with increasing intensity. Is this the big one, the final, winner-take-all battle? The American public is nervous with anticipation; everyone remembers the catastrophe at the French fortress at Dienbienphu fourteen years earlier where the French were vanquished and humiliated. President Johnson summons his Joint Chiefs of Staff and does something unexpected and unprecedented. He directs them to sign a statement that will be made public asserting that Khe Sanh "could and would be held at all costs."[29]

You are a Chief of Staff and know such an assertion at this stage is not only unjustified, it is absurd. But you know your president is, in this way, providing the veneer of reassurance to the American people that will keep his approval ratings up and his domestic agenda on track while simultaneously covering his a** politically in the event things go sour. Do you sign? What valued principle will you step on here? Will it be the military judgment and advice you deem best and are expected to provide as a Chief of Staff, an officer loyal to his corps and sincere about his professional honor (and which would likely entail your resigning your commission)? Or your loyalty to the president because he is your commander-in-chief? What gives (in the sense of caves-in)? What gives is one's best military judgment and advice. All the chiefs signed that document.

At the Tip of an Iceberg

Possibly the tip of an iceberg, the following is a particularly egregious example of integrity failure. It is that of the combat lieutenant who, confounded by an unseen enemy who repeatedly kills his men and slips away, lets his emotion of helpless rage inform and direct him. Putting a vengeance-driven sense of justice ahead of what is right, Lt. William Calley, on March 26, 1968, initiates and leads a massacre of between 347 and 504 unarmed South Vietnamese civilians at My Lai including women, children, and elderly men, in whose midst some Vietcong may or may not have found sanctuary.

Arguably, other soldiers stained by the ripples of this crime ought to include not only those who participated, and those who abetted its subsequent cover-up, and even those who were witnesses but did nothing, along with those

---

29. Michael Herr, op. cit. p. 105.

judges of the court martial that rendered a judgment that found that only one soldier, Lt. William Calley, merited punishment. (Arguably, President Nixon, too, belongs on this list. He reduced Calley's punishment to three years of house arrest in 1974. This occurred several months before Nixon resigned from office to avoid impeachment hearings for his own criminal misconduct.)

A search of the National Archives reveals that the massacre at My Lai along with the practice of cover-up and deception is, indeed, the tip of an iceberg. Other war crimes were neither reported nor investigated. Christian Appy describes one document in particular, a letter written in 1970 by a sergeant who'd participated in a military operation, Speedy Express. In his letter, the sergeant asks that the Pentagon investigate that Operation. At issue is the response of military units to orders demanding high body counts. This resulted in innocent civilians being killed in high numbers, such as by arbitrarily declaring certain areas free-fire zones even though few enemies were suspected there, and air strikes and artillery called in on villages even though no one from that place had fired a shot at any U.S. troops. The numbers of civilians killed in this way, this sergeant wrote, added up to My Lai numbers multiplied many times over.[30] (Civilian casualties from Operation Speedy Express were subsequently determined to be between 5,000 and 7,000.)

Appy's report continues,

"A Pentagon lawyer deemed the sergeant's charges plausible, and investigators located him for further investigation. Before they could proceed, Westmoreland shut it down."[31]

Appy further notes that,

"No top commanders openly rebelled against the body count obsession, even though many harbored serious private doubts about its effectiveness and morality."[32]

However, not all participants in these killings became thugs. Some were, themselves, traumatized. Private Paul Meadlo was there at My Lai. He refused Lt. Calley's order to murder the sixty or so Vietnamese men the private had gathered together under Calley's order and who were squatting together in a group. Calley insisted and became angry when Meadlo demurred. He gave Meadlo a direct order to shoot and kill them all. Private Meadlo reluctantly attempted to obey but quickly broke down. In tears, he handed his weapon

---

30. Christian G. Appy, op. cit. p. 181.
31. Ibid.
32. Ibid. p. 181.

to another trooper who continued the shooting. Once back home Meadlo found that most townspeople supported his (limited) participation in that crime. "Things like that happen in war," one veteran of WW II and Korea assured him. "They always have and they always will." One has to obey one's officer, they all reassured him. His parents, however, saw differently. He was a good boy, his mother recalled. "He fought for his country and look what they done to him – made him a murderer!"[33]

Inside the White House

President Johnson has boxed himself into a corner. The way to victory risks bringing China and the Soviet Union into the fray. The way out, withdrawal, means losing, and that, to him, means bringing America's international standing, its reputation and leadership, to an end. Paralyzed by this bind of being unable to win and unwilling to lose, but also unwilling to switch America's energy and focus exclusively on its domestic issues – in other words, to stop trying to maintain both Vietnam and his Great Society agenda as co-equal priorities – something has to give. Something *does* give – his integrity. When our planes are shot down in raids against the North, it isn't the inadvisability of sending planes ill-equipped for Southeast Asian weather systems, raids that oblige flying low under the clouds and in easy range of the enemy's modern and sophisticated anti-aircraft weapons, that is the problem. It isn't our limiting the targets that we'll bomb, either. Anti-aircraft batteries and missile defenses, for example, provided by the Soviet Union, are off-limits to our pilots until there's certainty there will be no Soviet technicians in the area meaning, until that system is up and running and ready to take on American airmen, we leave them be. That's not the problem. And it isn't our ally's security system's egregious breaches that allow the enemy to know that the planes are coming that is the problem. It is our pilots. To President Johnson it's our pilots at fault. To his generals who bring him negative reports he'll jibe with an expression like, "it looks to me as if the boys are inexperienced."[34] The president, at whose desk the buck is supposed to stop, slickly passes that buck back down the line. Integrity failures are everywhere. (I include the Joint Chiefs who, in this instance

---

33. Ibid. p. 150.
34. H.R. McMaster, *Dereliction of Duty: Lyndon Johnson, Robert McNamara, The Joint Chiefs of Staff, and the Lieu That Led To Vietnam* (New York: Harper Perennial, 1997), p. 265.

anyway, allowed the president to get away with unjustly faulting airmen.)

It is like a perverse counterpart to Eisenhower's "falling dominoes" prediction. Instead of a series of countries falling victim to communism, it's now a series of leaders who are fighting communism falling victim to corruption of integrity. But, so far, there are no blemishes worth noting on our national identity, our narrative shield, thanks to continuous and determined burnishing and misdirection along with blaming and passing the buck. (Does anyone today know, let alone care, that we secretly dropped more than 2 million tons of bombs on a neutral country during that war, more bombs than we dropped on Germany and Japan during World War II, and that killed or maimed thousands of children, farmers, and other civilians there? Does anyone today know, let alone care, that we're still paying indemnity to Laos?)

On the University Campus

Remember the time Ohio national guardsmen were ordered to advance toward anti-war protesting students on their Kent State University campus with rifles with fixed bayonets pointing forward? At some point, their commanding officer ordered those guardsmen to open fire. President Nixon had already denounced such protesters as "bums." Ohio governor, James Rhodes had already likened them to – declared them, actually – as worse than Nazi brownshirts and communists. What is a guardsman to do? There had been a riot the day before and protesters had set fire to the ROTC building on campus. Ought the guardsman aim into the air? Discharge one's weapon into the ground? Or should one aim and fire at a specific student engaged in threatening behavior? Or fire without aiming. Four students are killed, and nine wounded, many of whom are non-political bystanders or between classes and curious about what was going on. One student protester who'd been shot and killed had been standing more than 100 yards away from the guardsman who shot him. The national guard general reassures his shaken guardsmen that they had to do what they did, endorsing Nixon's position that such students brought it on themselves. No guardsman or leader is convicted of a crime. If we are O.K. with that outcome, even indifferent, how is that not cynical of us, and how does such cynicism not diminish our integrity?

In Our Streets

Construction workers in Manhattan are ordered by their employer to put aside their construction duties that day and, instead (and with pay), make a counter-march vis-a-vis a scheduled anti-war march. Despite the fact that more than a few of these hardhats marching with American flags are, themselves, opposed to the war, the construction workers as a group, and as if part of a plan, meet up with and physically assault the anti-war marchers.

At other locations, anti-war protesters ambush returning veterans, viewed as symbols of intolerable American policies. They target these men when the men are alone, unsuspecting, and unprotected. Then they aim and fire off their hateful and hurtful verbal shots. But, these are dutiful warriors who'd followed orders and displayed courage, duty, honor, and willingness to sacrifice in the service of their country; they're not policymakers. Some, like me, are likely anti-war themselves. So, which is the priority? Is it targeting Americans first (such as those citizens who answered the call of duty) or "America" first (meaning our elected leaders and their policies)? Should anti-war protesters march in the street carrying signs that will have negligible impact on national policies and bring limited personal satisfaction but cause no collateral damage to fellow Americans? Or should they, at any time and anywhere, march into veterans' faces for the immediately and personally satisfying experience of expelling anger, ire, and their sense of helplessness but at the cost of untold collateral damage to fellow Americans?

And what about those returning veterans, caught between honor and freedom, between celebrating the honor of military service, their corps, their nation, and their comrades-in-arms versus celebrating American freedoms that include the freedom to assemble, speak one's mind, and express one's derision, scorn, and rejection of the fighting man who'd dutifully put himself in harm's way to protect these same rights and these very protesters?

Especially egregious is what happens when the Chicago police are called in to face unruly, screaming, and taunting anti-war protesters outside the 1968 Democratic Convention Center. Ought the police try to impose order quickly and aggressively? Or, ought they approach with restraint if for no other reason than that this scene is being televised live and broadcast everywhere and the police and the city leaders are easily identifiable? The Chicago mayor makes his decision and the world sees protesters beaten and tear-gassed and the Mayor of Chicago, Richard Daley, at one point, screaming a crude, anti-Semitic slur at Senator Abraham Ribicoff of Connecticut, who is protesting the police beatings. The effort to impose order in the streets is not balanced by an equally relevant effort to respect the civil liberties of those people in the streets. Instead, restoring order replaces the civil rights issue altogether. It's a win-lose.

An attempt at compromise wherein each side has a chance to give a little is what one would hope and expect. America is famous for this approach, for seeking balance, insured by a constitution that protects from both the out-of-control mob and the dangerously powerful tyrant. In Chicago, any gesture towards such a win-win compromise was evidently overruled and bypassed by the mayor and his win-lose directive. The failure of civic leaders that day, to recognize the need for, and opportunity to, display for the world to see, that we're Number One as custodians of that balance and as defenders of both rights and protections, dishonors us.

Towards the final years of the Vietnam War, we began to reap what was sown. The culture of spinning, dissembling, misinforming, lying, and blaming, along with a host of derelictions of duty and other kinds of integrity erosion and their affiliates, manageable dysfunction, began bearing fruit. We read about American soldiers putting comrades and missions at risk by drug use and disobedience of orders and even assassination of officers. This took us by surprise but, actually, it was the same wine only in new bottles. Likewise, when our leaders, toward the end of the war, seemed more concerned with blame-avoidance than statesmanship, that, too, was the same old wine. When President Nixon matter-of-factly violated American law with his bag of dirty tricks to further his political ambitions and then obstructed justice to conceal the truth, it was as if such misconduct for him was business-as-usual. Again, the same wine but in a new bottle.

In Our Heads

"Support the troops" was a frequent and earnest pledge. "I support the troops." We must support the troops." "Let's support our troops." But, while it was so easy to say, it was quite difficult to think about. If we meant supporting the troops over there, fighting, it meant seeing that they made it home safely, and, given our interminable stalemate status in Vietnam – the nuclear option clearly off the table – that meant withdrawal. But withdrawal meant that those who'd made the ultimate sacrifice had died in vain, that their deaths had no meaning. And if their sacrifice was to have meaning surely we had to oppose withdrawal. We had to advocate – at least stand for – fighting on, even as fighting on meant more American lives lost for a cause we could not win. Which was it to be? Would it be a betrayal of those who'd made the ultimate sacrifice for nothing? Or a betrayal of those still alive by our pushing them into the killing fields without hope, another meaningless tactical victory? So we repeatedly told ourselves and others that we supported our troops, whatever that meant and tried not to think too much about it.

APPENDIX II

CHAPTER 6: OUR VIRTUOUS BLIND SPOT: OUT OF SIGHT, OUT OF MIND

It was my political leaders
who showed me how to live with corruption successfully and honorably,
but not how to process and deal with it.

1. President Truman Involves Us in Vietnam in 1950

Context:

America's initial involvement in Vietnam arises out of a terrible quandary. We are facing two bad choices and have to decide between them; we are in a bind.

The year is 1950 and the French are still trying to recover their former colonies of Indochina that they'd surrendered to the Japanese in 1940. They are in their fourth year of fighting and their war is at a stalemate. France turns to America for help. But President Roosevelt, along with a majority of Americans, supporting a principle of national self-determination, has opposed returning newly liberated peoples to their former colonial status which seems to be what France has in mind, despite their providing "cover" for such intentions, their pseudo-sovereignty arrangements.

However, Roosevelt is dead and President Truman is focused on a real and imminent threat, the expanding grip of Soviet communism over Europe, now reaching into Asia. If we weren't old enough to remember the Red Scare of the 1920s, we were probably old enough in 1950 to appreciate the destructive impact of the Soviet agenda of a worldwide revolution. Instability, any instability, especially among newly emerging nations in Asia that had formerly been European colonies, by compromising Asian trade routes, for example, would impinge on Japan's post-war recovery. Should Japan's experiment as our democratic ally fail, given China's fall to communism, it isn't a reach to see Japan falling under the sway of a communist economic sphere. That would place our economy and, arguably, our national security at risk, at least insofar as successful global capitalism is considered essential for the growth of the U.S. economy. A limitation of trading partners and shipping lanes would interrupt that growth.

This issue is magnified by France appealing to us for help. They want us to help them break their stalemate fighting the communist-led Vietminh, League for Vietnam Independence, and hint that, if we don't provide them with aid, given their understandable reluctance to accept a re-armed (West) Germany, they'll have to reconsider their commitment to NATO, the North Atlantic Treaty Organization. NATO had been created for the expressed purpose of containing further expansion of Soviet communism, and containment is the policy Truman selected, his Truman Doctrine. Happily, the NATO Pact, aligning the WW II allies (now including an armed West Germany to the discomfort of many French) appears to be working. But, to aid the French in Indochina in the interest of a unified NATO in Europe would mean violating our principle of self-determination for emerging nations. As Truman, now the clear leader of the "Free World" avers in his 1949 inaugural, "The world looks to us for leadership."[35] Truman must choose.

Truman chooses to support NATO in Europe which means, of course, turning our back on an emerging nationhood in Asia, specifically Indochina. In July 1950, one month after communist North Korea invades the South, President Truman sends a ship with aid to the French in Indochina to help them defeat the Vietminh insurgents there. This has been a difficult decision for Truman but the risk of communist expansion in Asia has been judged to outweigh the benefit of being principled about supporting the full liberation of peoples of former European colonies.

Truman's argument is well-known. Only a year earlier – in 1949 – China fell to communists, and communist North Korea invaded South Korea only months before. Ho Chi Minh, the leader of the League for Vietnam Independence, is a Moscow-trained communist. Stalin may be grandiose in considering all the emerging, post-colonial era nations his prey, but he understands and respects strength and military strength is the only thing that has given him pause in Europe. It may just give him pause, too, in Southeast Asia. Stalin is assumed to be in control of all expansionist movements of

---

35. Harry S. Truman, XXXIII President of the United States: 1945–1953, *Annual Message to the Congress on the State of the Union*, January 5, 1949, in The American Presidency Project, www.presidency.ucsb.edu.

communism but Mao in China is still an unknown. Is he considering an expansion of communism into Indochina? If Ho Chi Minh appears to be losing his war or the anti-communist administration the French had put in place in the South begins taking over, will that trigger Mao's intervention?

In any event, Truman does not doubt that the Soviets are behind these efforts to expand communism in Asia as well as Europe. As his Secretary of Defense explains to him, his choice is between either supporting the Vietnamese state the French created in the southern portion of the disputed territory or facing the extension of communism over all of Southeast Asia and possibly beyond.

As a condition for our providing aid, the French promise they'll grant at least some token independence to their Vietnam state in the south. However, they default on that promise. Inexplicably Truman continues the aid anyway. It's as if we, the United States, the world's strongest nation economically and militarily at that point in time, care more about Western European security than does this one major European nation, France. We apparently do. Things are that fluid, unpredictable, and menacing and the U.S. is apparently that flummoxed. From this same state department report appear these remarkable revelations relating to that flummox: "Contributing to the initial U.S. decision to aid the French and to limiting the effectiveness of the U.S. program of assistance were, (1) setting impracticable preconditions for assistance upon the French, (2) the U.S. proclivity to accept a slender chance of success without weighing alternatives, (3) the suppression of alternatives leading to decisional circularity and reinforcement of existing policies, (4) repeated failures of the U.S. to bargain effectively with the French, and, (5) the vulnerability of the U.S. policy-making machinery to spoofing, particularly as regards U.S. credulity in accepting French information at face value and in being susceptible to "Red" scares."[36]

Alternatively, one might argue that we really didn't expect the French to win and that's why we drew the line at introducing U.S. combat troops. From this viewpoint our U.S. aid was meant to serve as a gesture, a response in kind to the French promise of pseudo-independent status for the Vietnamese people, also a gesture.

If there was one thing post-war emerging nations needed, wanted, and were ready for, it was friends. It was certainly not road-blocks to their quest for independence. If their choice of government was to be between

---

36. Ibid.

communism and capitalism – or, from their perspective, between socialism and imperialism – friends from the West were crucial.

What President Truman is looking at but not seeing, as he weighs his response to the French, are the people of the emerging nations themselves, specifically, the Vietnamese people. He certainly doesn't see Ho Chi Minh, the recognized leader of the Vietnamese people. In fact, no one in France or America does, as the policy behind the following State Department political review suggests.

"We have not urged the French to negotiate with Ho Chi Minh, even though he probably is now supported by a considerable majority of the Vietnamese people, because of his record as a Communist and the Communist background of many of the influential figures in and about his government.[37]

Truman doesn't recognize Ho's need for a friend in the West as relevant to our interests. He doesn't see that, arguably, Ho will need us as his friend more than we need him to be our friend, that Ho's determination to limit Chinese encroachment actually matches ours. The Vietnamese people, especially their history, not only hold the key to containing China, they are offering that key. A united communist Vietnam is in both our interests.

Truman, looking in their direction but focusing on "emerging nations," "Asians," and "communism," doesn't see Ho and the Vietnamese people and their dreams, fears, and determination. He doesn't notice that, the choice of governance between what we see as democracy and tyranny is, for them and notably for Ho Chi Minh, between self-governing and foreign control. In short, while Truman shows interest in them hearing and knowing about us, there is no interest in us hearing from them and learning about them, about Ho. Yet isn't this precisely what is called for? A policy evaluation of 1948 paradoxically highlights this issue of us listening to them and not the reverse by its conspicuous absence:

"We have not been particularly successful in our information and education program in orienting the Vietnamese toward the Western democracies and the U.S..... An increased effort would be made to explain democratic institutions, especially American institutions and American policy, to the Indochinese by direct personal contact, by the distribution of information about the US, and

---

37. State Department Statement of U.S. Policy Toward Indochina, 1948," in *Major Problems in the History of the Vietnam War*, Robert J. McMahon, Ed. (Cengage Learning, 2008), p. 51.

the encouraging of educational exchange."[38]

Truman doesn't notice the differences among and within these emerging nations, most notably Vietnam's traditional abhorrence of outsider control, and most especially their abhorrence of control by China towards whom they hold special animus. With former colonies already rife with hatred towards not only former colonizers but abetting nations as well, all in the West, it is especially important that Truman reverse that trend. But, for this to happen, he needs to see them if for no other reason than one day they'll be seeking membership in the new United Nations organization. Best they start leaning toward the West early.

The objective of U.S. policy regarding Indochina in 1948 seems honorable and worthy enough, an end to hostilities between the French and the Vietminh without compromising U.S. security. Likewise appearing honorable and worthy is attending to the relationship of the people of Indochina with Western powers. But here's where disrespect seeps in. America's view of their "cooperation" with the West, culturally, economically, and politically, feels more akin to obeisance to the West than "sharing" with the West, and our aim to raise their standard of living, for example, without identifying exactly what part of the way they live is a problem to them, highlights this imbalance of respect. The following disrespectful and deceptive State Department statement, part of an extended statement of U.S. long-term objectives in Southeast Asia, is instructive. One objective is, it says: "to prevent undue Chinese penetration and subsequent influence in Indochina so that the peoples of Indochina will not be hampered in their natural developments by the pressure of an alien people and alien interests."[39] The presumption here is that the Chinese are alien people with alien interests while the people in the West are not. This State Department perspective seems oblivious to the fact that we, the people of the West, are actually the "alien people," and that our Western cultural, economic, and political interests are the true "alien interests." The authors of this statement seem unaware that a unilateral rejection by the West of any concern about the penetration and influence of China into Indochina denies the people of Indochina their own agency in that decision, in what might arguably be their "natural development."

If being seen, acknowledged, and respected seems an obvious place to start, and Ho Chi Minh is generally understood and accepted as the foremost

---

38.   Ibid. p. 52.
39.   Ibid. p. 50.

nationalist leader in Indochina, and in any general election he would be the clear winner, shouldn't there be some contact with him? Since self-determination of emerging nations has been our repeatedly stated interest, wouldn't it behoove Truman to communicate directly with Ho? At least to feel out his intentions and size up his credibility firsthand? After all, as a later State Department review notes, "... Communist Ho Chi Minh is the strongest and perhaps the ablest figure in Indochina, and any suggested solution which excludes him is an expedient of uncertain outcome."[40]

Truman acts as if Ho's letter, five years earlier, reaching out for our friendship, was never received. It certainly was never acknowledged. Now, 1950, would be a good time for a face-to-face talk between Ho and a Truman representative, and acknowledgment that the letter would be a good starting point. After all, given that we had, at that point in time, a functioning cordial relationship with a communist Yugoslavia whose determined resistance to Soviet influence and whose neutralist stance seemed all we needed to know to be a friend – a Ho victory over the French followed by a communist Vietnam followed by a determined Vietnamese resistance to future Chinese influence – would appear to be both a realistic and acceptable outcome for U.S. interests. What worked in Europe should work in Asia as well.

The Cold War, as it is taking form at that time, is about posturing, message sending, and covert operations; the threat of a nuclear exchange being the elephant in the room. Yet, given this reality, and even if our default position is to be one of hatred of an evil and godless Ho Chi Minh and what he represents, does Truman's message to the people of Indochina seeking independence and, indirectly all peoples of emerging nations, really mean to say not only that we don't know them and don't feel the need to know them, but also we actually don't care to know them? Does Truman not see that a disrespectful and threatening posture vis-a-vis the people of the emerging nations everywhere is what they'll see? Maybe all they'll see?

Truman's principle focus is on NATO and Stalin's intentions now apparently reaching into Asia. Communist Chinese troops are on the border of Indochina and, if the communist insurgents in French Indochina are going to fail, Chinese troops, with a nod from Stalin, are certain to intervene. Since Truman is being blamed for the loss of China to the communists in the first place for his not sending in American combat troops to support the corrupt and decaying administration of Chiang Kai-shek, his response to such

---

40. Ibid. p. 52.

disapprobation, it seems, has to be a show of military strength, not nuanced statesmanship. As a result, Truman doesn't see that a Ho victory in Indochina would actually keep the Chinese out of Indochina, not draw them in.

Ho risked his reputation and status as leader of Vietnam's independent movement when he agreed to the pathetic arrangement he made with the French at the close of WW II wherein his Vietnam would be a truncated Vietnam with puppet status in a northern territory under continued French control until after the defeated Japanese withdrew. With this arrangement, Ho gave up his goal of a united Vietnam under his rule simply for the singular guarantee that the occupying Chinese in the north would be certain to leave. The French would see to that. The Allied agreement at Potsdam in 1944 had stipulated that the British would liberate the southern part of Indochina and disarm the Japanese while Chiang Kai-shek did the same in the north. But Ho understood China's covert intentions; they'd loot, steal, and stay. They wouldn't leave. As Ho explained to his disheartened followers regarding his agreeing to a part-country with puppet status: "Don't you realize what it means if the Chinese remain? Don't you remember your history? The last time the Chinese came they stayed for a thousand years. The French are foreigners. They are weak. Colonialism is dying. The white man is finished in Asia. But if the Chinese stay now they will never go." And then, this much-quoted declaration: "As for me, I prefer to sniff French sh** for five years than eat Chinese sh** the rest of my life."[41] Those Vietnamese sentiments were public. To Truman, they were as if invisible.

NATO in 1950 is embryonic, untested, and fragile. But France is heavily committed militarily overseas both in Indochina and Algeria. If NATO is to count on French divisions in Europe, someone has to pick up the slack for them in Indochina.

The balance of power in 1950 between East and West is delicate and fluid. In the event the communist-led Vietminh defeat the French in Indochina, an active French communist party would possibly be empowered to move to withdraw from NATO. This possibility, alone, like America's questioning French sincerity behind that veiled threat to withdraw from NATO, or simply our reassessing our judgment about France and its "pseudo-independence" deal with Vietnam, would make both America and NATO appear weak in Stalin's eyes. Keep in mind that it was only two years earlier that communists

41. Stanley Karnow, Vietnam, *A History: The First Complete Account of Vietnam at War*, (London: Penguin Books, 1983), p. 153.

seized power from a democratically elected government in Czechoslovakia in a coup d'etat and, since then, the Soviets have developed their own A-Bomb. The risk of a nuclear exchange with mutual annihilation is real and Stalin is not only firmly in power and paranoid, he is also unpredictable. Our need to stay focused for the sake of the "Free World" – for the sake of "civilization," as we termed it – here meets the unpredictability of an expansionist-minded Stalin and the unnerving toxicity of a Cold War between nuclear powers. Truman is focused. He backs NATO. NATO holds. There is no additional Soviet expansion into Western Europe.

Truman's Bind, Blind Spot, and Bright-Side

Truman's ethical bind is having to choose between justice and peace. By opting for peace, meaning making the integrity of NATO and the containment of Soviet Communism his priority, Truman looks without seeing the people of emerging nations who seek justice. Specifically, he doesn't see the Vietnamese people or their striving for self-determination following years of rule under a colonizing European power. He doesn't see that Ho Chi Minh's determination to limit Chinese encroachment actually matches ours. He doesn't see that a united (communist) Vietnam bordering (communist) China is actually in both our interests. His bright side? Truman ensures the survival of NATO. There is no additional Soviet expansion into Western Europe.

2. President Eisenhower Keeps Us There

Context:

The French are defeated and withdraw from Indochina. Our U.S. advisors to the French remain in Vietnam even though under no legal or moral obligation to do so, the Cold War outlook is that intense and compelling. With Vietnam now partitioned into a communist North and non-communist South, a temporary separation that both China and the Soviet Union hope will become permanent since neither is prepared for U.S. military intervention in Southeast Asia, President Eisenhower acts. He not only sets up a pro-American government in Saigon to which he sends, along with advisors, material and financial aid, he also approves violations of the Geneva Accords that he'd pledged to respect. We're seizing the initiative here and taking the advantage.

The pro-American leader we help install, Ngo Diem, has outstanding anti-communist credentials. Unfortunately, he has little else in his favor. Diem is seriously out of touch with his people, especially their expectations as a nation newly independent from foreign control. It is 1955 and Eisenhower's intention appears to be moving beyond Truman's policy of containment of communist expansion via the NATO Alliance, to his own unilateral approach. Perhaps U.S. economic as well as strategic interests in Southeast Asia are now weighing in. In any event, Eisenhower proposes to create out of this former colony of Cochin China, now South Vietnam – with no tradition of national unity, with diverse population, political factionalism, and historical intolerance for strong central authority – not only a strong, independent pro-Western nation but one that is expected to function along Western lines. Eisenhower is obviously viewing the partition of the Vietnamese territory into two parts, one communist and the other non-communist, not as a net balance (i.e. no single foreign power now dominates in Southeast Asia), but as a net loss (i.e. half the contested territory is now "lost" to communism). With his "falling dominoes" scenario in mind, Eisenhower sees this new balance as a threat to our friends as far away from Indochina as Australia, Japan, and India. Although Keenan's original concept of containment never specified that the show or use of military force be the only option, Eisenhower sees the U.S. showing military toughness to the communist world as a salient and effective measure, more so than addressing the unresolved political and economic issues by non-military means.

What happens next is that, with U.S. support, President Diem applies his own methods to ensure, not his acceptance by the people and their support for his policies such as by investment in and strengthening of the nation's economic health, but rather by his control over the people themselves. His measures initially work. Criminal gangs, long a feature of (and bane of) political life in Saigon under the French, are eliminated, along with most of the communist leadership and secret communist cells that remained in the South after the 1954 partition. The U.S. aid now coming in begins to allow a perception of a stable economy.

Diem's methods in establishing this control and that perception, however, are dictatorial, harsh, and repressive and quickly spawn objection and dissension. The emergence of this dissent, rather than prompting course correction on Diem's part, provokes brutal crackdowns with relentless persecution. This gives rise to a vicious cycle. Opposition to repressive policies provokes crackdowns which generate more opposition which obliges further crackdowns. There is no pretense at civil liberties now. Instead, it is a field day for the Viet Minh cadre remaining in the South who are quickly becoming active participants and leaders in this dissension, now an insurgency.

Diem's vision for Vietnam is clearly at odds with that of the Eisenhower Administration. His vision is not the "self-determination" and "democracy" the U.S. had in mind. Ironically, Diem seems to have taken a page from Eisenhower's play-book since, for Eisenhower, all nations that are not with the U.S. are considered against the U.S., meaning any nation seeking non-aligned status must be a pawn of Moscow, and therefore our enemy, and is treated as such. Likewise, for Diem. All dissidents in his jurisdiction are "communists" and are treated as such. They are silenced and/or eliminated.

David Anderson notes this process:

"By 1957 and 1958, terrorism and armed insurrection were on the rise in South Vietnam. This violence often represented retaliation and resistance to Diem's increasingly repressive regime. Most of these incidents occurred without the instigation of Hanoi. The DRV (Democratic Republic of Vietnam, North Vietnam) had not given up its objective of reuniting Vietnam under its rule but its leaders had ordered their southern cadres to be patient."[42]

By the end of the 1950s the dissidents, many of whom began as a loyal opposition to Diem, are no longer seeking reform. Now they're seeking regime change. Their identity as "loyal opposition," a staple of Western-style governments, simply does not compute in Diem's vision of a Confucian-guided system in which there can be only one truth. Dissidents are, by definition in this system, traitors. Leadership, according to Diem, is guided, not by consensus but by virtue, and Diem, a bachelor who has lived for years as a monk, literally, and still lives as an ascetic, assigns all the dirty work to a brother. Despite all this, on the surface, his nation appears sound.

In desperation, finally, beleaguered dissidents in South Vietnam plead to Hanoi for help. Hanoi however, at this time, still seeks to stay out of the troubles in the South. They have their own issues, such as maintaining control over an angry and restless population, now outraged at their government's abuses and excesses, especially their heavy-handed attempts to create, overnight, a classless society. So Hanoi again declines to step in and again counsels patience.

---

42. David L. Anderson, "The Tragedy of U.S. Intervention" in *Major Problems in the History of the Vietnam War*, Robert J. McMahon, Ed. (Boston, MA: Houghton Mifflin Co., 2008), p. 102.

But there's a problem. While Hanoi prefers that the insurgents employ propaganda and other destabilizing techniques rather than plunge into an armed conflict that could prompt a U.S. military attack on the North, southern resistance leaders, who face jail and execution, refuse to wait. They begin acting on their own, starting with assassinations, fire bombings, and small attacks on RVN (Republic of Vietnam) military units and outposts.[43] In this way, the dissidents force Hanoi's hand and Hanoi creates a Front organization, the National Liberation Front, that conceals from view its communist connection, and takes the reins. It is 1959.

By virtue of his declining to make our aid contingent on government reforms as he had initially insisted, Eisenhower abets Diem's repressive policies and civil rights abuses. This has consequences. Our goal of creating a strong, independent, and lasting pro-American nation in Indochina along the lines of a modern, democratic nation – a bulwark of freedom – is, so far, coming to naught. Also coming to naught is the South Vietnamese people's dream of independence with peace and justice. Their government in Saigon is hurting them and we, abetting this dictatorial government, are making new enemies simply by allowing our puppet to pull his own strings. Plus, we have still not protected the South from communist interference. In a later review of the ensuing debate about which should come first, crushing dissension and then addressing economic and social issues or vice versa, one notes an obvious blind spot; the debate gives no indication that any U.S. policymakers consider the option of "doing nothing and leaving the outcome in Vietnam to the Vietnamese."[44]

Eisenhower's goal of nation-building thus morphs into that of simply keeping a weak, ineffective, corrupt, and unpopular government, along with its facade of economic health and political stability, from collapse. And yet, as Anderson notes, "By the time Eisenhower left office in 1961, the goal of a noncommunist South Vietnam and the means of obtaining that objective – nation-building premised on the survival of the Diem regime – were so deeply ingrained in U.S. global strategy as to be virtually unassailable."[45]

The obvious detail that escapes Eisenhower's notice is, in his administration as in Truman's, the people of South Vietnam themselves. These are the people on the receiving end of Eisenhower's decisions, now the casualties of his

---

43. Ibid.
44. Ibid.
45. Ibid. p. 103.

stumbling nation-building campaign. These are the people whose allegiances are critical to success. It is these casualties that are arguably driving the insurgency that threatens the facade of stability. Like Truman, Eisenhower makes no personal connection with Vietnam's leaders, neither North nor South. He never hears a Vietnamese spokesperson articulate, face-to-face, the complex realities they are facing. His one meeting with Diem is, as the Pentagon Papers notes, "largely ceremonial." This source goes on to note: "Similarly, his (Eisenhower's) system of having his staff sift through options did not help alleviate his problem of comprehending complexity. Indeed, the key staff member upon whom he relied for foreign policy advice, Secretary Dulles, generally accepted the single-minded fixation on Diem."[46]

In any event, crises are cropping up elsewhere around the globe during Eisenhower's administration, from the Taiwan Straits, Suez Canal, Lebanon, and Berlin, to Little Rock, Arkansas. And to his own health; his heart attack is in 1955. Following his recovery from this heart attack and return to a full workload, we read, "he gave little personal attention to the details of Vietnam which his staff presented to him as an issue that was being managed well. He accepted those optimistic assessments and, during Diem's 1957 visit, lent his voice to the chorus of praise for RVN's achievement."[47] The Vietnamese people, themselves, continued to be invisible.

But, even facades have their place and value. Diem's facade of stability works. The detail that's invisible to Eisenhower's critics is the effectiveness of that economic and political facade. South Vietnam's stability is bogus but it works. It proves convincing enough to maintain peace in the region. The fragile balance among competing powers in the neighborhood continue to hold.

Eisenhower's Bind, Blind Spot, and Bright-Side

Eisenhower's ethical bind is also that of having to choose between justice and peace. Opting for peace he seizes an advantage that ensures America's standing as the premier world power at the expense of the will of the majority of Vietnamese people and their preferred leader. Eisenhower sees neither the Vietnamese people nor Ho Chi Minh. His bright side? He oversees America's hegemony in Southeast Asia as peace is sustained there.

---

46. Ibid. p. 104.
47. Ibid.

3. Kennedy Digs Us in Deeper

Context:

Whereas containment based on a show of strength works to contain Stalin in Europe, it is the application of strength that works against Mao in Korea. Indochina, however, is different. South Vietnam has not been invaded by another nation. In fact, North and South Vietnam were meant to be only temporary "military regroupment zones" prior to general elections and unification. They became "nations" by default because general elections were never held. Now, South Vietnam is facing, not an invasion, but an internal adversary, an insurgency fueled by a corrupt and repressive Saigon government. South Vietnam President Diem's pro-American government requires serious reform if the communist-led insurgents of the South are to be neutralized. These reforms are essential. Diem refuses.

For Kennedy, new to his office and with a team that will be setting policies for a region that is to them, to varying degrees, "like some unknown land,"[48] there is much catching up to do. In the transfer of power, however, Eisenhower's team presented Kennedy's team with little in the way of thoughtful analysis of the problems South Vietnam poses or the pros and cons regarding alternative ways to deal with them. This was not a helpful orientation, suggesting that Eisenhower and his team were, themselves, stumped.

How does Kennedy respond to Diem's intransigence regarding reform? Instead of making our aid contingent on those reforms such as the long-overdue land reform and elementary civil rights, Kennedy focuses on enhancing the military strength of Diem's army. He does this despite knowing such a focus will prioritize the protection of the Diem regime and its control, making the people's issues secondary. Kennedy also continues to provide financial aid knowing it will be used, not so much to develop businesses and industries for a sound economic base for South Vietnam as to line pockets and import consumer goods.

In short, rather than containing any further encroachment of communism into South Vietnam, these policies simply continue the unpopular Saigon government's alienation from its people. Instead of investing to ensure a healthy free market economy and security with justice for the people, if not

---

48.   Robert S. McNamara, *In Retrospect: The Tragedy and Lessons of Vietnam* (New York: Times Books, 1995), p. 32.

by the rule of fair laws (a Western concept) then at least a rule by fair laws of their ruler (Diem's non-Western equivalent), and instead of developing a broad base of popular support along the way, the Saigon government does the opposite. Kennedy's strategy of focusing on the insurgency and insurgents who must be beaten back and chased away rather than on the dysfunctional governance that is alienating the people and fueling their insurgency, is backfiring. Vietnamese people are caught between two onerous options.

Kennedy's priority and primary motivation seems to be the importance of showing strength to the outside world, showing we're serious about containing any further spread of communism in Asia. Kennedy seems intent on demonstrating to Premier Khrushchev of the USSR that he, Kennedy, isn't weak, as if to deter Khrushchev from further high-risk adventures. (Kennedy had already acquiesced to the Berlin Wall and, in good faith, collaborated with Khrushchev to end a destabilizing civil war in Laos by sponsoring a "neutral" coalition Laos government, a good outcome. But both moves were perceived by Khrushchev as a sign of weakness.) And, although Kennedy has the good sense not to throw good money after bad by not intervening on behalf of anti-communist Cuban rebels caught on the beach at Cuba's Bay of Pigs after that mission had been compromised, it turns out that Castro knew they were coming, and was prepared. Kennedy is here making apparent that his show of strength in Vietnam might actually be more for Khrushchev's edification than South Vietnam's benefit.

But Khrushchev isn't Stalin. True, he is committed to supporting liberation movements in place of fomenting worldwide revolution, and true, he is now in competition with, not allied to, China, in his seeking to co-exist peacefully with the West. But, also true, Khrushchev has his pride and national image to protect and project. So, if it's to be about displays of strength between him and President Kennedy, that's what it will be about. (Kennedy will pay for this apparent show-of-strength ploy the following year when Khrushchev, in his show of strength, introduces missiles to Cuba that will be aimed at the U.S.)

Kennedy's option to focus on his image on the international stage seems to have pushed what is before him in Indochina into his blind spot, namely, a South Vietnam governance and economy that has become the poster-child, not for democratic capitalism as originally intended, but for anything but. It's not the communist promoters and their Vietcong activists that are threatening the capitalistic way in South Vietnam. It's the sorry example that is being peddled. The example of South Vietnam's economy, now based on foreign handouts with clear inequalities of wealth and justice, along with the persistent internal bickering among its out-of-touch leaders and a growing population of suffering and disaffected citizens who've already inspired one attempted coup against their leader, seems to be proving Stalin and his communist creed correct. In their predictions of capitalism's future, Stalin and his communist creed have predicted that capitalist nations of the West will, as always, bicker and fight among themselves until, as in the past, they become violent, turn on one another, and collapse. One has only to wait.

But what does a healthy free-market economy have to do with the communist threat? This. At the core of the conflict between democracy and totalitarian communism, between East and West, between the USSR and the U.S.A. – the Cold War – is precisely this face-off of economies. These were the only available and potentially viable alternatives, post-World War II, for the recovery of devastated European nations and for post-colonial emerging nations. These two paths to recovery were, back then, in competition, and final choices were up for grabs. What was obvious was that co-existence between the capitalist and communist ways (or, from the other side, the imperialist and the socialist ways) was not possible insofar as the communist way demanded worldwide revolution. How were people to choose? The capitalist way was messy, with strengths and weaknesses, but it did have a track record. The communist way was an ideal that had never really been tested.

Like his predecessor, Eisenhower, Kennedy abets the abuse, oppression, corruption, and decay of an unpopular dictator-led Saigon government, now held up on display, with its toxic and embarrassing excesses presented as a model of democratic capitalism. Kennedy is seriously discrediting his product. Remarkably (in retrospect), Kennedy doesn't appear to see that it's the hearts and minds of the consumers, the people of South Vietnam, that are needed to win this competition, not land. He doesn't seem to see that it's the Saigon government, itself, that is killing its cause. We may be speaking of sponsoring democracy and freedom but it is global capitalism, the engine that drives our strength, authority, and influence, that makes such a goal viable. The point is that the purveyors of the communist message are not what is interfering. What is causing most of the dissension and causing the dissidents to not only grow in number but shift their advocacy from that of a change *in* government to a change *of* government, is the Saigon government's display of venal imperialism. In Kennedy's endorsing and promoting such a corrupt and decaying system that is hurting its own people who need redress, he is discrediting his non-communist option. He does not see this.

Kennedy's Bind, Blind Spot, and Bright-Side

Kennedy's bind is having to choose between promoting a strong Republic of Vietnam economy or a strong Saigon government. He chooses a strong government and, as a result, an American supported undemocratic South Vietnam government expands its power over its people while abetting rather than reforming their corruption-riddled economy. It becomes, not the poster child for democratic capitalism as originally intended, but the opposite. The weak Vietnam economy, now based on foreign handouts with clear inequalities of wealth and justice, can't help but demonstrate that Stalin and his communist creed about capitalism's inevitable demise, are correct. Kennedy seems not to notice that he is seriously discrediting his product before the world and sowing seeds for continued dissension with growing ranks of dissidents. His bright side? In continuing this proxy war in this way, Kennedy is assuring the world that the Cold War tensions will be played out here in Southeast Asia where the nuclear option is farthest from anyone's mind. This kicking of that can further down the road inside a Third World country is what buys time for everyone to find their way back from that nuclear armageddon.

4. Kennedy Burns a Bridge Behind Us

Context:

It is 1963. The Cuban Missile Crisis is behind us. We've shown toughness and Khrushchev has withdrawn his missiles. By this time our mission in Indochina has morphed from creating a bastion of freedom in South Vietnam to that of simply keeping a weak, ineffective, fragile, corrupt, and increasingly unpopular Saigon government from collapsing – defeat avoidance. This is not what we'd signed on for, excusing and shielding this government from its own people who demand change. Finally, an egregious display of religious intolerance, a brutal crack-down on Buddhist dissidents, becomes a flash point in President Diem's relationship with his people and a tipping point in his relationship with the U.S.

In these critical times, two opportunities arise. The first is Diem's initiating talks with Hanoi about forming a Federation wherein South Vietnam becomes a "neutral" state and the government a coalition government that includes communist representation. This would allow Hanoi to rid itself of intrusive

Chinese aid and Saigon to do the same regarding the U.S. presence. President de Gaulle of France, especially, is not only advocating this resolution but urging it. Kennedy dismisses this as a ruse. He doesn't see this as a potential opportunity for us to withdraw with honor. The second opportunity relates to the growing rift between the communist superpowers, the USSR and China. They are no longer the strong monolithic foe they'd been. Kennedy dismisses such reports of a Sino-Soviet rift as communist propaganda.

What Kennedy does, in the context of repeated conferences with advisors and listening to their divided opinions and recommendations, is signal a group of ARVN (Army Republic Vietnam) generals, who have sent out a feeler, that the U.S. would not interfere if the generals ousted President Ngo Diem in response to the unfolding turmoil Diem is fueling. When the generals move forward with their plotting, Kennedy doesn't interfere. He doesn't even inquire about the replacement for Diem the generals have in mind, as if he needn't vet any such replacement nor even gauge what the replacement's political policies will be and how those will work with ours, as if such post-coup details are immaterial to him.

What is going on here? The Sino-Soviet split, an opportunity for the U.S. to strengthen its position, remains officially under our radar and the Federation option is regarded, not as an opportunity to withdraw with honor, but as betrayal. Kennedy doesn't see opportunities here. Were these even discussed, let alone debated? Apparently not. In McNamara's words, "Ironically, amid all the debate, we still failed to analyze the pros and cons of withdrawal."[49] He later adds about the Federation with neutrality option, "If de Gaulle – who had as much to lose as we from such a blow to the West – could accept neutralization, why could not we?"[50]

McNamara's notes of the many conferences Kennedy held with advisors on the matter of that coup proposal, a group that included military and ambassadorial staff, show their focus to be intense, troubled, divided, and profoundly anchored in unquestioned Cold War verities. For example, questions were never raised at these conferences about whether the Chinese and Soviets were still an ideological monolith, or whether a non-communist South Vietnam truly was critical to American national security, or whether a communist South Vietnam would actually trigger communist takeovers of nations throughout Asia and beyond. McNamara's notes reveal an indecisive

---

49. Ibid. p. 63.
50. Ibid. p. 113.

and uncertain President Kennedy struggling with what to do about an obstructionist ally, a mounting crisis, divided advisers, and conferences with those advisors that go in circles. In that context, what falls into Kennedy's blind spot is the fact that this box he is in is not only cardboard (i.e. the "monolithic" alliance between Russia and China is warped and collapsing), it has an actual opening. The "neutral" option for South Vietnam is like a door that would allow Kennedy to step out. That, too, is never seriously debated as an option in those conferences. The invisibility of such opportunities for Kennedy is highlighted by his subsequent assurance to the press at a November 14 news conference in Honolulu, twelve days after Diem's assassination, that our objective is still "to bring Americans home and permit the South Vietnamese to maintain themselves as a free and independent country."[51] Kennedy's default position is still that it is the South Vietnamese people's war to win or lose.

Keep in mind that, only the year before, Kennedy and Kruschchev together brought their nations up to the very brink of nuclear war, and both men now know, because they've been briefed in horrifying detail, the consequences of a nuclear exchange. (Both men were reported to have been shaken by the revelation that both the Soviet Union and North America would be destroyed.) Also, keep in mind that a key detail of the resolution of the Cuban Missile Crisis has been kept out of the headlines from the American people, namely that both men blinked; both men backed down. It was precisely this pseudo-secret that enabled Americans to appreciate and savor the relief, confidence, and pride that came when Kruschchev agreed to withdraw his missiles. How many of us appreciated the relief, confidence, and pride that the Soviets must have felt when, in exchange, Kennedy withdrew our missiles from Turkey that were aimed at Moscow. The withdrawal of our missiles from Turkey was not only kept low-key, it was deliberately delayed to minimize any linkage Americans might make to the Cuba Crisis resolution.

With his stepping back from the brink over the Cuban missiles, it's safe to assume Kennedy wished to avoid a repeat crisis and is likely to have drawn the following conclusions. The rift between Soviets and Chinese, the so-called Sino-Soviet Split, was likely to widen and deteriorate further because its core was an ideological issue, not easily remediable. For the U.S. to have taken interest and acknowledged this weakening of the other side would surely have

---

51. Vito N. Silvestri, Becoming JFK: *A Profile in Communication* (Connecticut: Praeger, 2000), p. 239.

generated discussion among us along with proposals of how we might seize the advantage. In that event, Beijing and Moscow would surely have considered not only a defensive posture but a united defensive posture, one obliging a temporary healing of their split. But, assuming a firm determination to avoid another nuclear face-off, Kennedy would likely have been thinking more about backing away from another such brink than moving towards it again. Following the resolution of the Cuban Missile Crisis did we, the people, not feel more relieved than victorious, more sobered than exultant? Surely Kennedy shared that reaction. But what he knew and we didn't was that a compromise was won that day, not saber rattling. And maybe we were deliberately kept from knowing because we were not yet ready to embrace such an alliance, such a contract with an "evil and godless" foe that would expose us as "soft on communism."

This brings us to the Federation option, to Diem's flirting with this private rapprochement with Ho Chi Minh. This assuredly would have alarmed us, the American voters, cued as we were to reject such accommodation as treachery. So, (hypothetically), if Kennedy were to lead America away from the brink, and considering how we'd all been cued to look first at the military option for all confrontations, he'd need time. To buy that time and be able to lead us in this new direction, Kennedy would first need to be re-elected in 1964.

Kennedy signals he will not interfere with a military coup to remove President Diem. Diem is our ally, but he is also an obstacle to our purposes as well as an enemy of his people, the majority of whom view him as having no legitimacy as a leader and who is continually generating fodder for the communist's propaganda machine along with replenishing Vietcong ranks. So, why should Kennedy interfere when the Vietnamese military who, in response to the clamor of their people, sets to remove this dictatorial and abusive leader, this government that will not change itself and that is abetting the growth and spread of the communist front organization? Kennedy's non-interference with this proposed coup, like his behaving as if the details of a post-coup arrangement were immaterial, makes sense if "self-determination" enters the equation. It makes sense if after re-election Kennedy intends to exit South Vietnam and leave its political destiny to the South Vietnamese people, a safe as well as acceptable "spin."

In fact, Kennedy does mention this intention to colleagues, quietly and low-key, as if testing the waters with an eye towards deniability. Had Kennedy, instead, left a paper trail or had included his vice-president in his confidence about such an intention, such information could have put his re-election in jeopardy. How could such a "rumor" not have leaked? In any event, if Kennedy was to be re-elected, and with South Vietnam arguably in the hands of people better suited in many ways to represent them than Ngo Diem, Kennedy could declare that the United States did its duty and then withdraw honorably and with support of the American public. South Vietnam's political future in their own hands would have also reassured Americans that self-determination was still a valued American principle.

Kennedy's Bind, Blind Spot, and Bright Side

Kennedy opts for the principle of religious freedom over that of loyalty to a long-time ally, following President Diem's severe crackdown on protesting Buddhists. What seems to disappear into a blind spot is the consequence of potentially losing this Southeast Asian anti-communist ally. Kennedy appears to ignore the Sino-Soviet split, apparently not seeing here the opportunity there for the U.S. to strengthen its position in Southeast Asia. He appears to ignore the Federation option, not seeing the opportunity to withdraw from Vietnam with honor. But appearance can be deceiving. Arguably, it was with withdrawal in mind that Kennedy ignored the Sino-Soviet split. Wouldn't taking advantage of that split have risked pushing these two communist behemoths together again, against the West? And, arguably, it was with withdrawal in mind that he disparaged the Federation option. To have endorsed it would have made him appear "soft" on communism and he would never have been re-elected and Americans needed time to prepare to accept a U.S. withdrawal from Vietnam. Re-election would provide that time. He would first, of course, need to float such a notion as a trial balloon. Is that what he was doing when he made mention of a withdrawal option to a government colleague? Did his decision not to bring Lyndon Johnson, his vice-president, into his confidence serve as insurance against such a leak? We'll never know. Such a bright side was cancelled by Kennedy's assassination.

5. President Johnson "Americanizes" the War

Context:

In 1963 President Johnson's interests are primarily political. They are about re-election in 1964 and, probably, his domestic agenda once re-elected. But priorities and inattention are not why Johnson never develops a clear grand strategy for the Vietnam War. A clear and successful strategy had, after all, eluded his predecessors. (Defeat avoidance is not a strategy.) When Johnson steps into the presidency after Kennedy's assassination not only does he have serious catching-up to do – he'd been kept out of the loop under Kennedy – the national security team he'd inherited has serious work to do as well. They were seriously divided and the situation in Southeast Asia was not only worse, it was also desperate and unraveling. Complicating matters, foreign policy matters were well outside Johnson's comfort zone. They were well outside what Johnson knew best and understood and had experience managing.

Johnson had been a successful and influential senator. Pushing, prodding, elbowing, calling up, calling on, and getting a consensus were his forte. A towering and powerful man who usually got his way and got things done, he was strong that way. But now, as president and facing a complicated political problem in Vietnam that called for a political solution, he was uncertain and anxious. His advisors were divided over recommended courses of action. If the Vietnam conflict could only be resolved by a negotiated settlement and the North wasn't talking, what should you do? Without a stable non-communist Saigon government we'd never be able to withdraw. Johnson had to find a way to stabilize this Saigon government currently on the brink of collapse. At the same time, he had to persuade Hanoi to come to the negotiating table. Continued U.S. passivity would only abet the inevitable defeat.

Johnson agrees with the Joint Chiefs that the situation calls for action. Convinced that Hanoi is operating under the aegis of Moscow, meaning they haven't a horse of their own in this race, Johnson sees a way to spoil that relationship and make Hanoi respect us and attend to us. He'll pressure Hanoi, and show we can hurt them while simultaneously increasing our bargaining power at the table. A negotiated settlement on our terms will follow and we'll pull out. (Just how a bombing campaign will force Hanoi to the table isn't clear. Likewise, the specific U.S. objectives that might or should be achieved at that negotiating table aren't drawn up and made clear, either.)

With this in mind, Johnson reduces the priority of social reform and civic action projects currently underway in South Vietnam, their political objective being winning the hearts and minds of the Vietnamese people to their government, in favor of military measures, specifically bombing the North. It won't get American hands dirty. The "Tonkin Gulf Resolution" has given him a green light. But when bombing doesn't have that desired effect and he continues bombing anyway he is obliged to put American combat boots on the ground in the South to protect those air-bases. It seems that Johnson's track record of dominance with control, his familiar modus operandi and comfort zone is here bumping up against a real risk of failure (and a genuine fear of right-wing criticism). Those realities trump the sort of humbling and chastening compromise options that are sometimes necessary to resolve knotty political issues like the ones before him. One would think that admitting you are wrong or mistaken, at least to your staff and supporters and the public, and then "punting," as it were, by inviting congress to weigh in and share the fame or blame, would be a respectable and honorable place to start. Not for Johnson. As Doris Kearns notes in her biography of LBJ, "The experience of a long political career had confirmed him in the belief that there were no differences that could not be settled by upping the ante."[52] Johnson opts to press on.

How does the North respond to our bombing? With China's help, they repair the damage and relocate manufacturing activities and personnel. How do they respond to Johnson's escalation in the South – his introduction of combat troops? With escalations of their own. They single out American facilities for the attack. We are crossing the line here from being advisors to becoming combatants. The Vietnam conflict is now officially "Americanized." It is 1965. It is America's war now. How does the American public respond? The American public becomes polarized.

The subsequent course of this war, now our American War, will be that of escalation and counter-escalation, always ending in a stalemate and always at increased levels of violence. In the ensuing years, Johnson will repeatedly be asked to explain his strategy, and his explanations will repeatedly fall short of clarity. It is as if what he is trying to do here is either not fully clear to himself or must not be permitted to be fully clear to the public. It is as if defeat-avoidance and kicking the can further down the road are the best we can do. The part that Johnson does make clear is that he absolutely will not be the first president to lose a war. Withdrawal is absolutely off the table. Or, from Kearns' perspective, so insecure is Johnson in foreign affairs and dependent on the foreign affairs experts he has inherited and now needs, and whose disapproval he truly dreads, his strategy boils down to avoiding making a serious error. It isn't seeking to accomplish something important anymore.

---

52. Doris Kearns Goodwin, *Lyndon Johnson and the American Dream* (New York: St. Martin's Griffin, 1976) p. xi.

His objective is merely not appearing "foolish or incompetent."[53] Privately, Johnson is flabbergasted. Why can't the U..S. beat a "piss ant country" like Vietnam! We can't even find a tipping point wherein they will come to the table and beg for settlement. Johnson is incredulous. Doesn't everyone have their tipping point, their weakness?

Johnson is described as intelligent and hardworking as well as, at times, either open or devious, loving, compassionate, gentle, and generous, or mean, scheming, and cruel. He is described as a towering, powerful, and paradoxical figure."[54] He is also described as needy, thin-skinned, easily hurt, intolerant of being alone, and insecure. Johnson is a complex person.

A primary source of Johnson's strength and dominance is his awareness that everyone has their weakness. As McNamara observes, "He took every person's measure. He sought to find a person's weakness, and once he found it, tried to play on it."[55] However, as with many of us, he can easily see something in others that he can't see in himself. This is Johnson's weakness. He can't see that his aversion to the appearance of weakness in his administration, party, or nation, is personal. As a result, he doesn't see that his political sensibilities and judgments have become contaminated by this personal issue.

Johnson is unable to see the corrupting effect his insecurities have on his political instincts and their contaminating effects on his policy deliberations, an example being his fundamental default position regarding any foreign policy deliberations or decisions regarding Vietnam that posit total withdrawal and being permanently off the table. For his generation of males, the traditional American striving seems aimed at being Number One, the top position, that of "winner," the bottom being for "losers." (The striving to be "All You Can Be" is still years away.) The influence of that striving is arguably why, for all his talk of wanting a way out of his bind and believing negotiations to be the ticket, when an opportunity arises and the ducks are lining up and a talk with the enemy about mutually de-escalating in play, and wherein his halt to the bombing of the North is the key to starting this ball rolling – the so-called "Marigold" option – Johnson unexpectedly decides not to postpone the bombing of the North scheduled for the days before the talks are to begin. Worse. When the U.S. planes attack,

---

53. Ibid. p. 256.
54. Robert S. McNamara op. cit. p. 98.
55. Ibid. p. 99.

they go after new targets around Hanoi, itself, the site of the talks! When asked years later why he did that, why he put the kibosh on that meeting, Johnson instinctively pointed to his concern that it might be interpreted as a sign of weakness.[56] Johnson could just as easily have pointed to the Joint Chiefs' argument for not stopping the bombing, namely that any pause would risk enemy troop movements and that would put our men at risk.

The withdrawal option is a personal anathema. It doesn't compute for Johnson as a political alternative or geopolitical strategy. He won't even discuss or debate the idea. When his vice-president suggests he consider such a discussion Johnson bans Vice-President Humphrey from policy meetings. Likewise for the Joint Chiefs of Staff whose mantra is becoming something like "we either go all out to win (with a nuclear strike on the table) or withdraw." Johnson, not surprisingly, sees to it that Chiefs are kept outside the loop. They are given only limited access to deliberations and intentions. It's as if Johnson's self-esteem and international standing are here conflating, just as his self-esteem has conflated with national security.

No surprise that McNamara's accounts of the cabinet meeting deliberations repeatedly note the absence of serious debate or careful discussion regarding the growing list of questions that call for answers. It's as if there is, under the radar, a silent culture of censorship. Questions go unaddressed, such as, will nations opting for neutrality inevitably fall to communism? Ought we prevent that? What would be the political, financial, and human cost of our intervening militarily? Does the "falling dominoes theory" still hold true?

In his memoir, McNamara claims to be puzzled about why there was no serious debate in his group as if his boss hadn't made clear not only that some topics were off the table, but that there would be consequences for putting them on the table (and, as if his advisors' unwillingness to raise that issue weren't for this reason; namely, that it traces back to Johnson, himself, and his insecurities).[57] Withdrawal from Vietnam, for Johnson, represents weakness and failure. For Johnson, exiting Vietnam doesn't compute as a sign of an acceptance of reality or political wisdom, those other kinds of manly strength and courage. Instead, for Johnson, withdrawal means losing, and losing means being a loser, and a loser is at the bottom. What else can a real man do but silence discussion?

As to why his subordinates didn't debate and discuss this among themselves

---

56. Ibid. p. 249.
57. Ibid. p. 154.

at least, if not face-to-face with Johnson, there is no obvious answer. Would it have felt disloyal or seemed disrespectful? Would it have been interpreted as an intrigue and subterfuge by Johnson? In any event, Johnson is unable to see that the help he needs on this, of all matters, is sound political advice, not indulgence or reassurance. With this in mind, not surprisingly, his advisors behave at times more like enablers and apologists than advisors.

Johnson came into office inheriting a deepening crisis that was more complicated than it had been and with advisors divided on the correct analysis and required action. He was well outside his comfort zone with this Vietnam conflict. Despite these handicaps, Johnson was determined to push his domestic legislation forward and redirect the nation in a positive direction. (His signature Civil Rights Act of 1964 and Voting Rights Act of 1965 are that legacy.)

Furthermore, in his concern about doing the manly thing, his masculine self-image informing his national security judgments, he was not an outlier. The ideal of the American male hero is the action hero. The valence between manliness and power and strength is arguably stronger than between, say, manliness and wisdom and judgment. How could Johnson or any man in that role not be mindful of his image as a man? Actions, for Americans, do speak louder than words. And if it's in our national myth (if not our genes) that this is so, of course the dots connect toughness with defense and protection, and defense and protection with overcoming fear, vulnerability, and insecurity, and the male's perceived physical strength as the determinant. The point is, Johnson's concern about image as an American male (along with his personal sense of himself as a man) is warranted.

Johnson's Bind, Blind Spot, and Bright-Side

Johnson faces a choice between the virtues of reforms in health and civil rights for all Americans and the sanctity of truth. He chooses health and civil rights and, with that in mind, and his need for both hawks and doves in Congress to endorse his Great Society domestic legislation, he knows he must finesse his relationships with his opposition, both at home (congressional) and abroad (communist insurgents and their sponsors). To succeed he must be mindful of the weaknesses of his foes. His awareness of his own weaknesses must take a back seat. As a result, he never lets himself see wherein his aversion to the appearance of weakness contaminates his political instincts and policy deliberations. He never lets himself see where his personal insecurity conflates with national security and contaminates his decisions as Commander-in-Chief. In short, Johnson doesn't see that the advice he most needs from his Secretary of Defense is sound political advice, not personal reassurance and indulgence. This large man has a large blind spot. His bright side? Johnson sees to it that all America dodges the stain of quitter, appeaser, weakness, and failure.

6. Secretary of Defense McNamara Imposes his Losing Strategy of Gradualism

Context:

Writing of the beginnings of his career in government, Robert McNamara, in his autobiography, *In Retrospect: The Tragedy and Lessons of Vietnam* (1995), notes his naiveté and blunders stepping into the role of Secretary of Defense under President John Kennedy in 1960 after having been president of the Ford Motor Company. "I had hay in my hair," he recalls.[58] His was a steep learning curve and there would be speed-bumps, but he prevailed. His memoir helps us. It begins with his personal history, his early years, as background. His portrait of his family and the early years provides insight into the person he becomes. In this way, McNamara shares how this background shaped the principles that inform his later motives and decisions. We're not surprised to read, then, about subtleties he misses in the ways of Washington, like not catching on when his leg is being pulled. But, as he'd done in grade school, he stays on his feet and aims for the top. What begs the question is why, when he becomes secretary of defense and sees the dearth of Southeast Asia experts in government service owing to the discouragement, if not purge, of such sources from government service in the early 1950s, he makes no effort whatsoever to restore and gather that expertise to at least cultivate potential specialists as government assets. He surely understood from the start that knowing what went before, the setting and background, helps one understand and manage the present.

As Secretary of Defense, McNamara's immediate tasks are huge and important. As a cabinet officer, he is responsible, no longer to the Ford family, a board of trustees, or investors, but, in his view, to one man, the president of the United States, his single source of authority and the only

---

58. Ibid. p. 18.

one to whom he is truly accountable. But matters outside that focus, that don't get his full attention as a result, occasionally throw curves in his path anyway. For example, he recalls, "I had entered the Pentagon with a limited grasp of military affairs and even less grasp of covert operations. This lack of understanding, with my preoccupation with other matters and my deference to the CIA on what I considered an agency operation, led me to accept the (Bay of Pigs invasion) plan uncritically. I had listened to the briefings leading up to the invasion. I had even passed along to the president without comment an ambiguous assessment by the Joint Chiefs that the invasion would probably contribute to Castro's overthrow even if it did not succeed right away. The truth is I did not understand the plan very well and did not know the facts."[59] (McNamara voted his approval for that operation.)

Fast forward to 1965. Lyndon Johnson is now president, the Vietnam conflict has worsened, a stable Saigon government is nowhere in sight, and LBJ has Americanized the war. He's done this latter move as part of a plan to persuade Hanoi that Saigon will never be allowed to fall and to provide them with the incentive to negotiate with us. We'll demonstrate we can punish the North to their breaking point, the point beyond which their ability and will to continue supporting the insurgency in the South fail, and they'll seek a negotiated settlement with us. Johnson's primary interest, of course, remains his domestic agenda. He wants to be done with this scary, expensive, and bedeviling Vietnam distraction. In this setting, and given the proxy nature of the conflict and as a subtext for signals exchanged between the U.S., the USSR, and China, McNamara develops a plan whereby the message to Hanoi and to Moscow, and Beijing as well, will be clear: America wants a negotiated settlement with Hanoi. America does not want a wider war.

To this end, the U.S. bombing of the North will be incremental, at less than full strength or intensity. We'll be looking and listening for signals from Hanoi. We're keeping the lines of communication open, as it were. McNamara is here presuming that there actually is a tipping point beyond which the enemy will cry "Uncle" (and it'll be to Sam, not Ho), the expectation being that when Hanoi seeks negotiation it will be soon and on our terms. Johnson's "Great Society" agenda is already expensive enough. Also presumed is that a loss of South Vietnam to communists continues to endanger U.S. national security as well as the security of many other nations; not only those in the region but those beyond. So intense is Johnson's focus on Vietnam, it's as

---

59. Ibid. p. 22.

if the setbacks China is experiencing vis-à-vis its relations with Russia, the emergence of a new Indonesia with an anti-communist government, and growing dissension inside China that is turning that nation inward – the Cultural Revolution will begin the following year – have had no impact on our Falling Dominoes prediction.

This approach or strategy to bring Hanoi to the negotiating table is called "Gradualism" by the administration. The Joint Chiefs of Staff, who have strong objection, call it "Restraint." For them, this is no way to win a war, giving the enemy time to recover after hitting him. Plus, it risks sending the opposite message, namely that the U.S. is ambivalent and uncertain. In fact, so dissatisfied are Joint Chiefs that they conduct war games to gauge the most realistic outcome. These games determine that, in the face of this gradualism approach, (1) the North and Vietcong will escalate and attack U.S. installations and personnel, (2) air strikes will not deter the enemy, (3) we will come to underestimate Hanoi's resolve and, eventually, (4) American resolve will flag. This is eerily prescient.[60] (Johnson never receives these results of those Pentagon war games.)

Despite the significant loss of planes and men with no response from Hanoi, Johnson goes ahead with this strategy. Even after it becomes clear that the bombing is not meeting its stated objectives of hurting the North enough to impede their ability and will to continue supporting the insurgency in the South, Johnson continues bombing. The Joint Chiefs, despite having no faith in this gradualist, restrained approach, accept their Commander-in-Chief's directive and continue to implement it. (A myth will emerge among the military that the war, beginning to be referred to now by many as "McNamara's War," could have been won but for such "civilian meddling.")

In his memoir, McNamara identifies his objects of inattention, those in his blind spot. There are many. They include his not seeing the context, the history, and culture of his adversaries even though they are in his face, their fierce nationalist aspirations, dedication, patience, tolerance for pain, and staying power to name the obvious ones. Even though seeing this might have provided access to the enemy's fault lines as well as strengths just as his own background, revealed years later in his memoir, he exposes to readers his fault lines as well as strengths. Other objects in his blind spot are the strategies

---

60.   H.R. McMaster, *Dereliction of Duty: Lyndon Johnson, Robert McNamara, the Joint Chiefs of Staff, and the Lieu That Led to Vietnam* (New York: Harper Perennial, 1997), pp. 89–90.

that made him a successful manager in the private sector, the work that was his life and daily bread for twenty years. It was as if those were suddenly invisible to him as Secretary of Defense. In his words (regarding meetings with General Westmoreland and staff) years later, "Although I questioned these fundamental assumptions (e.g. that Vietnam is critical for U.S. security, that a communist victory in South Vietnam would cause a domino effect and other nations would fall to communism, etc.) during my meetings with Westy and his staff, the discussions proved superficial. Looking back, I clearly erred by not forcing – then or later, in either Saigon or Washington – a knock-down, drag-out debate over the loose assumptions, unasked questions, and thin analyses underlying our military strategy in Vietnam." McNamara goes on to ponder, "I had spent twenty years as a manager identifying problems and forcing organizations – often against their will – to think deeply and realistically about alternative courses of action and their consequences. I doubt I will ever fully understand why I did not do so here."[61] (He is talking here about this blind spot.)

McNamara is pointing out that that is no way to run a business. It was certainly not the way he ran his business. Yet that is precisely the way he ran the Department of Defense for President Johnson. He claims he's at a loss to account for this. If he's telling the truth about not fully understanding this "invisibility" – meaning this is not likely about lack of courage, political expediency, flawed thinking, or ignorance – a good part of the reason is likely the combination of intense focus on an impossible task joined to a powerful emotional valence toward that task. It is almost as if a secret agenda was to provide a stressed and insecure Johnson with the shield of steady reassurance from a calm, confident, and positive advisor. With this in mind, one recalls in his memoir that he had been selected as president of the Ford Motor Company in part to protect Henry Ford II from repeating his father, Edsel's, sad end at the age of 49. Edsel Ford, the only son of Henry Ford and president of Ford Motor Company from 1919 to his death in 1943, was believed to have died young, according to Edsel's wife, Henry Ford II's mother, because of the stress of that Ford Company job. That job was a killer, his killer. McNamara was well aware of that managerial subtext. Recalling Mrs. Ford's reaction to his termination notice (she was shocked and upset) he

---

61. *Major Problems in American Foreign Relations, Volume II: Since 1914. Seventh Edition*, Documents and Essays Edited by Dennis Merrill, Thomas Paterson (Belmont, CA: Wadsworth, Cengage Learning, 2010, 2005), p. 420.

recalls: "She was determined that her son would not suffer a similar fate and had looked to me to shield him."[62] In his memoir, McNamara will mention the many times Johnson called upon him to take action in areas outside his Defense domain, beyond his assigned role, at least once in an agitated state,[63] and McNamara's responding by doing whatever was necessary to satisfy such requests. By highlighting the confidence and trust that he merited in that relationship with his president, it's as if McNamara never needed to take his reflections to the next level, the level of questioning the need for such a relationship, and what his acquiescence signified.

McNamara's Bind, Blind Spot, and Bright-Side

Facing a choice between his allegiance to America and allegiance to President Johnson, between his duty regarding national security and his duty regarding his president's emotional insecurity, McNamara puts the President first. As a consequence, his devotion to his president's needs and sensibilities conceals from his view the fierce nationalist aspirations of our adversaries in Vietnam. McNamara does not see, for example, the enemy's dedication, patience, tolerance for pain, and staying power. He does not see that the strategies that made him a successful manager in the private sector, such as the aptitude for challenging loose assumptions, unasked questions, and thin analyses and his readiness for debate, are sorely needed here. He does not see that his steady reassurance to his stressed and insecure boss is interfering with both of them – him and his boss – doing their jobs. His job was as advisor to that boss, not enabler. His bright side? McNamara's highly criticized "Gradualism" strategy ultimately does ensure that the U.S. never provokes China into entering the war. Again, the world dodges nuclear Armageddon.

7. General Westmoreland Pursues a Controversial Policy of Attrition

Context:

In 1964 President Lyndon Johnson appoints General William Westmoreland as MACV Commander of the 16,000 American advisors and, the following year, after U.S. combat marines have landed and been tasked

---

62. Ibid. p. 13.
63. Robert S. McNamara, op. cit. pp. 99-100.

with defending key airfields, Johnson asks Westmoreland to direct a buildup of U.S. combat troops. At this point, Vietcong holds the initiative in parts of South Vietnam, the U.S. counter-insurgency efforts (or "pacification") are on hold, ARVN forces are on the defensive, and the fall of Saigon appears imminent. The situation is difficult and complicated. Johnson's objectives and directives for Westmoreland are likewise difficult and complicated.

Washington wants Westmoreland to convince the Vietcong and Hanoi that the insurgents can't win. He is directed to accomplish this by defeating the Vietcong and interdicting Hanoi's contribution of men and material to the insurgency, doing both with minimal U.S. casualties. He's not to provoke the Chinese. There's more. His troops must not cross into neutral Laos or Cambodia. In all this, Westmoreland will buy time for Saigon to put its political house in order because there can be no final victory without a stable Saigon government. In any event, this effort is also intended to strengthen the U.S. military position in the field, in the event of peace negotiations.

Where to start? On the one hand, Westmoreland understands that the key to defeating the insurgency is the people. They need to feel secure and safe if they are to give their allegiance to the Saigon government and dare to deny the Vietcong any sanctuary. On the other hand, Westmoreland knows that the Americans are better equipped and prepared than ARVN to interdict North Vietnamese regulars coming south along the Ho Chi Minh Trail or to meet them head-on in their sanctuaries in the countryside. Accordingly, he opts to address both by assigning ARVN the counter-insurgency tasks while he takes on the rest.

Westmoreland understands the political dimension of the war. But, given the constraining and contradictory objectives of his mission, he opts for a military policy that will impact both the Vietcong in the South and Hanoi in the North. He'll deny the Vietcong the numbers they need to continue operations in the South. He'll seek out, engage, and destroy Hanoi's large forces already there. He'll take on these enemy main forces both at their base areas and in the field. His intention is to kill them faster than they can be replaced. Once this program of attrition reaches the enemy's "tipping point" wherein North is unable to keep up with losses in the South, the Vietcong will fail as a military force and Hanoi will lose heart and seek a negotiated settlement with the U.S. That is the plan.

The measure of success of this attrition policy, the sign that we are, indeed, pushing the enemy towards his tipping point, our indicator that the U.S.

is winning, will be body counts, the numbers of enemy killed. For reasons that are still debated, Westmoreland deliberately underestimates the enemy numbers of fighting men in his calculations. Some say it's to ensure that his accumulated body counts repeatedly point to progress by enhancing the percentage of enemy killed. In any event, with those positive indicators of progress along with the obvious approval and support of the president, Westmoreland pursues this policy, these Search and Destroy operations, for four years. There are no other signs of progress or success other than those numbers plus Westmoreland's steadfast certainty that there will be a tipping point.

In fact, there is every evidence that the enemy's tolerance for pain and loss exceeds anything Westmoreland and Washington ever imagined. Hanoi does not lose heart, the Vietcong continue their operations, and the numbers of young men in the North coming of military age continues, by far, to exceed any number of dead bodies Westmoreland puts up. If the objective is to destroy Hanoi's fighting spirit while boosting the morale of ARVN, neither succeeds. In fact, it's the opposite. Hanoi's determination grows in the face of American might while ARVN becomes even more willing to let the Americans do their fighting. Still, Westmoreland doggedly puts up his "winning" numbers and, at every opportunity, points out that, under his leadership, the U.S. is winning every battle.

Westmoreland's policy and judgment are finally exposed as a failure when, having convinced Americans that we were winning this war, he appears totally unprepared for the enemy's TET Offensive in January 1968. Worse, when the enemy begins that offense with a diversionary attack in a remote area in the far north of South Vietnam, Khe Sanh, to draw U.S. and ARVN forces away from the cities, Westmoreland suspects that this assault at Khe Sanh might be the "big one," our Dienbienphu, and sends more troops up there. Then, when the General Offensive begins shortly afterward and 30 provincial capitals are attacked simultaneously, Westmoreland mistakenly interprets that as a diversion.

It was only ten weeks earlier that Westmoreland assured an American audience that America would prevail in this war, that there was light at the end of this tunnel. He is replaced as Commander of MACV that June.

Westmoreland is so intent on pushing enemy casualties beyond Hanoi's tolerance to their "tipping point" he doesn't see that other body count. Ours. He doesn't notice the impact of this other body count on the American public. The numbers of Americans killed are climbing. While his field officers are pleased to report enemy dead in the thousands after an engagement, Americans at home are wincing at the report of American dead in the low hundreds. An obvious question becomes, how is it that Westmoreland sees an enemy "tipping point" where one doesn't exist but doesn't see an American "tipping point" that is growing under his nose? And, as the number of American dead climbs so does the noise in America's streets. 1968 is the bloodiest year for Americans. There are 14,600 U.S. battle deaths.

There is something else in Westmoreland's blind spot. Early in his tour as commander, he wrote in planning documents that the security for the people in the hamlets and towns was key to defeating the insurgency. Given that awareness, when his policy of attrition was backfiring, why did he not course-correct? Why did he not stop trying to find and kill Vietcong and return to providing security for the hamlets and villages, at least enough to win the people's approval for their government? It's as if he didn't see the backfire of the attrition policy and didn't see that hearts and minds of the people were still the key to achieving our objectives, a stable and lasting non-communist government in Saigon. In any event, Americans at home saw that backfire on the nightly TV news, sometimes literally, watching U.S. troops set fire to villagers' homes with their zippo lighters. If they were doing this to minimize the risk of ambush – their orders being to search each and every house for the enemy – then such Search and Destroy operations were worse than ineffective. They were counter-productive. The collateral damage to people as well as property was not just severe, it was severe, ongoing, and self-defeating.

Ironically, the policy of attrition worked at the start, in a way. It kept the enemy's main forces away from the big cities and wrested the initiative away from them. That the policy had limitations appeared only after the enemy, respecting U.S. superior mobility and firepower, began steering its large units clear of further head-on combat with Americans.

Westmoreland's Bind, Blind Spot, and Bright-Side

For our Vietnam ally to prevail and America to "win," the hearts and minds of the Vietnamese people must stand behind their government and the enemy must withdraw. For General Westmoreland this is his bind: He can concentrate on only one of these objectives. He can either get the people to step up by supporting and protecting them or get the enemy to step down by protecting the Saigon government from the insurgents and their communist allies from the North. He opts for making the enemy step down and protecting the Saigon government. His tactic will be attrition. He'll kill the enemy in numbers they won't tolerate; he'll push them to their tipping point. They'll sue for peace. His measure of progress will be the count of enemy dead. What he doesn't see, of course, is that the hearts and minds of living people, the Vietnamese civilians in the countryside are, arguably, more critical to victory than enemy dead bodies. He also doesn't seem to see that the greater the American presence and role, the lesser the Vietnamese army's incentive to fight and sacrifice on their government's behalf. He doesn't appear to see that there may be no enemy "tipping point," while an interminable loss of American life and treasure may broach our own. His bright side? His policy of attrition, his Search and Destroy Operations, do succeed in wresting the initiative from the enemy and keeping their main forces away from big cities, thus possibly (and paradoxically) reducing overall American losses. And consider: Had Westmoreland shifted the American focus from Search and Destroy Operations to civic action which would have obliged providing security for civilians in their villages and hamlets, this would have placed American troops in fixed, defensive positions which would well have put Americans in the enemy's cross-hairs.